SHAPERS OF CHRISTIANITY

SHAPERS OF CHRISTIANITY

Brief Sketches of
Twelve Outstanding Christians
From Across the Ages

Nick Needham

THE BANNER OF TRUTH TRUST

THE BANNER OF TRUTH TRUST

Head Office
3 Murrayfield Road
Edinburgh, EH12 6EL
UK

North America Office
610 Alexander Spring Road
Carlisle, PA 17015
USA

banneroftruth.org

First Published 2025

*

ISBN
Print: 978 1 80040 523 3
Epub: 978 1 80040 524 0

*

Typeset in 11/15 Adobe Garamond Pro at
The Banner of Truth Trust, Edinburgh

Printed in the USA by
Versa Press Inc.,
East Peoria, IL.

Foreword

Reading church history has the potential not only to educate and inform, but also to encourage, challenge, and warn. Nick Needham has written extensively on the history of the church,[1] and this brief but richly engaging series of pen portraits focuses on men who have made significant contributions to the life and well-being of Christ's church. Dr Needham not only informs us as to why these men are worthy of being remembered, but also highlights their theological significance and the lessons we can learn today from their wholehearted commitment to Christ and the spread of his kingdom.

Dr Needham relentlessly reminds us that history is *His-Story,* the story of God's saving purposes in this world. This is a necessary, even vital, reminder that the unfolding of history is not haphazard, or determined by powerful personalities and socio-economic events. Our God reigns.

IAN HAMILTON
Professor of Historical Theology
Westminster Seminary UK

[1] See his multi-volume series, *2000 Years of Christ's Power* (Grace Publications Trust and Christian Focus Publications).

Contents

Introduction

The apostle Paul tells us in 2 Corinthians 4:6 that Christ is the human face of God. In similar fashion, godly individuals are the human face of church history.

In this series of studies, I give some brief sketches of twelve Christians from the past two thousand years who stand out for their human interest and theological significance. I have not always made obvious choices; hence my portrait of Theophylact from the Middle Ages, Peter Martyr Vermigli as representative of the Reformation era, and Tikhon of Zadonsk from eighteenth-century Russia. Perhaps Francis Turretin from the seventeenth century will be equally exotic to some (even though he really deserves to be better known, at least to Reformed readers).

I hope these sketches will help to kindle a spiritual interest in God's people and God's work across the ages.

Some of the material in chapters 1–10 has been adapted, with kind permission, from volumes 1–5 of my *2000 Years of Christ's Power,* published by Christian Focus.

NICK NEEDHAM
Dingwall, March 2025

I

Irenaeus of Lyons (flourished AD *175–195)*

> He was both man and God, so that he might suffer for us as man, and have compassion on us as God, forgiving us our debts in which we had become debtors to our Creator … Therefore, just as we were made debtors to God through a tree, we gain the forgiveness of our debt through a tree.
>
> (*Against Heresies* 5:17:3)[1]

For biblical Christians, the primary shapers of Christianity are (or ought to be) the prophets and apostles. Yet it would be perilous to deny that after the apostolic age, God has continually blessed his church with gifted people who have shaped the Christian understanding and practice of prophetic and apostolic teaching. In this short series, we shall look at some of these post-apostolic shapers of Christianity. We do this in the conviction that it is a healthy

[1] From my *Daily Readings: The Early Church Fathers* (Fearn, Ross-shire: Christian Focus, 2017), reading for February 20.

exercise. One of the great sins of the modern era is what C. S. Lewis called 'chronological snobbery': the belief that 'no doubt we are the people, and wisdom will die with us' (Job 12:2). On sober reflection, however, there seems no good reason to privilege the modern church with the fullness of all wisdom. Whatever wisdom we possess is very likely, at least in part, an inheritance from our ancestors in the faith, and it would be grievous to dishonour their labours by ignoring them. In addition, we may well find that in becoming acquainted with them, we catch some glimpse of God's truth and glory that was evident to them, yet which we perhaps do not see so clearly. Studying our Christian past can in this way become an eminently practical and spiritual discipline.

The first post-apostolic shaper of Christianity we meet is Irenaeus of Lyons, often hailed as the first great biblical theologian after the age of the apostles. Ethnically and culturally Greek, Irenaeus was born into a Christian family in Asia Minor sometime in the early second century. We do not know his birth and death dates, but he flourished as a Christian leader roughly between AD 175 and 195. Part of his significance lies in the fact that in boyhood, Irenaeus sat under the teaching ministry of Polycarp, Bishop of Smyrna, who himself in his youth had been mentored by the apostle John.[2] This chain of spiritual transmission holds enduring

[2] In the first few centuries of the Christian era, each local church had its own bishop, and all bishops were seen as essentially equal. In fact a bishop was little different from the Presbyterian understanding of a pastor.

fascination: John taught Polycarp, Polycarp taught Irenaeus. Irenaeus tells us that Polycarp's chief joy in the evening of his life was to describe his fellowship with John:

> I remember the things that happened in those times more clearly than the events of recent years. For what we learn in childhood, growing with our minds, becomes part of us. I can therefore describe the very place where the blessed Polycarp would sit when he preached his sermons, the way he would come in and go out, the manner of his life, his physical appearance, the very sermons he preached to the people, and how he used to relate his fellowship with John and the others who had seen the Lord: how he would tell us what they said, and the things he had heard from them concerning the Lord, His miracles and His teachings. Polycarp had received all these things from eyewitnesses of the Word of life, and he told us all these things, in keeping with the Scriptures. I listened intently to these things at the time, by God's mercy, and I noted them down, not on paper but in my heart, and constantly by God's grace I ponder them faithfully.

As a young man, Irenaeus moved from Greek Asia Minor to the city of Lyons in southern France. A spiritual bond connected Asia Minor and Lyons, since missionaries from Asia Minor had founded the churches of southern France. At this juncture in its history, the church in Lyons had a bishop from Asia Minor named Pothinus; Irenaeus was ordained as one of his presbyters. In AD 177, a violent wave of persecution engulfed the churches of Lyons and Vienne, and many believers were martyred, including Pothinus. It seems that Irenaeus was away in Rome during this outburst of anti-Christian fury, thus surviving the fierce tribulation. When the persecution had died down, Irenaeus went back to Lyons, and the church—in accordance with the democratic traditions of congregational life in those days—elected him as its new bishop in Pothinus' place. Irenaeus continued in office as Bishop of Lyons until his own death, which took place in roughly AD 200.

Irenaeus' position in Christian history is assured through his authorship of a lengthy treatise usually known simply as *Against Heresies* (its longer and more accurate title is *A Refutation and Overthrow of Knowledge Falsely So-called*). The book has come down to us intact, albeit mostly in a Latin translation. There is nothing quite like it for telling us about the standard beliefs of Christians in the second century, and about the great threat to apostolic orthodoxy in that period, namely the Gnostic movement. Irenaeus also wrote a smaller work against the Gnostics called *Proof of the Apostolic Preaching,* whose text was long thought lost, but the manuscript of an Armenian translation was discovered in 1904. (For more about Gnosticism, see below.)

Several facts about Irenaeus emerge from his anti-Gnostic writings. He was clearly a learned man, familiar with the ancient Greek classics of philosophy and poetry. He exhibits a comprehensive grasp of the Old Testament, and an intimate knowledge of most of the writings that came to be canonised as the New Testament.[3] He also shows himself fully acquainted with the various Gnostic sects and their distinctive doctrines. Further colour is added to our portrait of Irenaeus when we realise that there may have been a strongly personal element in his anti-Gnostic campaign: he had a boyhood friend, Florinus, with whom he had grown up in Smyrna, both having sat at Polycarp's feet. As an adult, however, Florinus had forsaken apostolic Christianity, becoming a disciple of the influential Gnostic teacher Valentinus of Rome. Irenaeus penned a long epistle to Florinus, exhorting him (in vain, alas) to return to the biblical faith, and Valentinus is the Gnostic whose doctrinal system Irenaeus principally critiques in *Against Heresies*.

Irenaeus' polemic against Gnosticism, and in favour of apostolic Christianity, can be summed up as follows:

(i) He rejects the central Gnostic claim that they were the unique custodians of a secret knowledge (*gnosis,* the Greek term for knowledge), essential to salvation, and allegedly passed on privately to Gnostic leaders by Jesus and the apostles. This claim was radically undermined, Irenaeus argues, by the embarrassing reality that none of the countless Gnostic sects saw eye-to-eye about what this secret knowledge

[3] The canon of the New Testament was still in flux in Irenaeus' day, with seven of its writings still disputed among the churches: Hebrews, James, 2 Peter, 2 John, 3 John, Jude, and Revelation. It would not be until the fourth century that consensus finally emerged on the canonical status of these seven disputed writings.

was; each had their own peculiar version. Allied to this, Irenaeus documents the fact that there were many churches known historically to have been founded by the apostles, or where the apostles were known to have taught. None of these 'apostolic churches,' however, were proclaiming any so-called secret Gnostic knowledge. On the contrary, they were all united in teaching the same biblical gospel, which contradicted Gnostic beliefs. This line of argument becomes progressively weaker, the further in time one gets from the apostolic period; but in Irenaeus' day, scarcely a couple of generations from the death of the apostle John, it had significant force.

(ii) Irenaeus demonstrates by careful biblical exegesis that—contrary to Gnostic belief—the God of the Old Testament, and the God of the New Testament, are the same God. (Gnostics routinely 'demonized' the Old Testament deity, setting him in stark antithesis to the supposedly superior New Testament God, a common view in our own day.) Irenaeus also argues that salvation does not come, cult-like, through the impartation of a so-called secret knowledge. Rather, humanity's redemption has been secured on the open field of history, through the life, death, and resurrection of Jesus Christ as God incarnate. The Creator has entered his world as one of his own creatures, taking upon him the role of a Second Adam, who by his perfect obedience has reversed and nullified the transgression of the First Adam. We see here how important it was for Irenaeus to tie together Old and New Testaments as a single coherent story.

(iii) Irenaeus defends the goodness of creation. It is not, as Gnostics claimed, the evil and ugly product of some inferior and foolish deity, but the glorious handiwork of the heavenly Father made known in Jesus Christ. We are 'fearfully and wonderfully made' (Psa. 139:14). He also affirms strongly that Christ truly took flesh, became a true human being, truly suffered and died, and truly rose again. This was in refutation of the Gnostic belief that the heavenly Redeemer could have had no genuine involvement in crude earthly matter. On the contrary, Irenaeus maintains, the heavenly Redeemer's union with earthly matter—with our human flesh and blood—is of the essence of his redemptive work.

We see in Irenaeus a theologian-apologist of mighty stature. We may disagree with him here and there (this will be true of any theologian from any era), but his achievement in setting forth apostolic Christianity in detail against the great seductive error of his day—Gnosticism—gives him a noble rank in the defenders of the faith and the expositors of Holy Scripture.

2

Gregory of Nazianzus (AD 330–390)

> Picture the Trinity as a single pearl, the same on all sides, shimmering all over. If any part of the pearl is damaged, the whole loveliness of the precious stone is gone. So when you dishonour the Son in order to honour the Father, the Father doesn't accept your honour. How can the Father glory in the Son's dishonour? Likewise, if you dishonour the Holy Spirit, the Son doesn't accept your honour. For although the Spirit doesn't come from the Father in the same way as the Son, yet He comes from the same Father. Either honour the whole or dishonour the whole, and so have a consistent mind! I can't accept your half-godliness. I would have you altogether godly.
>
> (*Oration* 37)[1]

The fourth century is often considered the Golden Age of the Early Church Fathers, owing to the sheer intellectual and spiritual brilliance of that century's Christian thinkers in expounding the faith doctrinally and practically. Among

[1] From my *Daily Readings: The Early Church Fathers*, reading for March 10.

its most influential figures were the Cappadocian Fathers. This was a group of three theologians from the Roman province of Cappadocia in Asia Minor—Basil of Caesarea, his brother Gregory of Nyssa, and his friend Gregory of Nazianzus. Once the famous Athanasius had passed from the scene, the Cappadocian Fathers led the church in rejecting and vanquishing the heresy of Arianism (which held that the person of Christ was not truly divine, but the greatest of God's creatures), and in giving clear expression to the doctrine of the Trinity.[2] Of the three Cappadocians, Gregory of Nazianzus came to be the most treasured by following generations. Greek-speaking Christians reverentially called him 'Gregory the Theologian,' as if he were the first true theologian after the apostle John.[3]

Gregory grew up in a Christian family, and as a student in Cappadocian Caesarea[4] met the young Basil of Caesarea, the two becoming intimate soul-friends. After the pair had studied and plundered for Christian use the treasures of ancient philosophy in Athens, the birthplace of Western thought, Gregory was then ordained in 362 as a presbyter in Nazianzus, his home church pastored by his father. Practical

[2] For my fuller account of this, see *2000 Years of Christ's Power* (Fearn, Ross-shire: Christian Focus, 2016), vol. 1, ch. 8.

[3] In the Greek East, the term 'theologian' had special reference to the doctrine of the Trinity. The apostle John was held to be the first great theologian in that sense, and Gregory the second.

[4] So named to distinguish it from various other Caesareas in the Middle East.

church life, however, did not appeal to Gregory. He was a sensitive introvert, unenthusiastic about the often sordid struggle of fighting Arians on the public battleground of church politics. Gregory's soul longed for solitude, where he would compose pensive poetry. Each has his own gift: Basil proved superb in the gladiatorial arena of ecclesiastical politics, but Gregory's contribution lay elsewhere, in his thoughtful eloquence harnessed in service to Christological and Trinitarian orthodoxy.

Despite his aversion to up-front church leadership, in 379–81 Gregory was briefly bishop of the little Trinity-confessing congregation in the Eastern capital city, Constantinople, where Arianism reigned supreme. He was, one might almost say, bullied into accepting this position by Basil and other churchmen. Reluctantly acquiescing, Gregory took up residence in Constantinople, in a villa provided by his cousin, which Gregory transformed into a chapel (the official church buildings were occupied by Arians). He nicknamed the chapel 'Anastasia'—resurrection—in the hope that the Trinitarian faith might undergo a resurrection there, in a city so besotted by Arianism. Indeed, the proverb that 'the past is another country' is nowhere more colourfully illustrated than in fourth-century Constantinople, where the popular passion for theology stuns and baffles a modern mind accustomed to total indifference on the topic. As another of the Cappadocian Fathers, Gregory of Nyssa, commented on Constantinople in his day:

> The whole city is filled with such people, in the public squares and markets, at crossroads, in the streets and alleyways. If you ask someone to give you some small change, his answer is to philosophize about the Begotten and the Unbegotten. If you go into a baker's shop to buy some bread, the shopkeeper gravely responds that *The Father is greater than the Son*. If you ask your servant whether the bath is ready, you have to rest contented with his assurance that *The Son has been generated out of nothing*.

Gregory's hope that Trinitarian faith might be reborn in the Eastern capital was realised. His most enduring fame to this day rests on the sermons he preached in the 'Anastasia' villa in defence of the Trinity, the *Five Theological Orations*. Gregory was always an enthralling preacher, perhaps surpassed only by the celebrated John Chrysostom in his 'pulpit' eloquence (although they didn't have pulpits in those days—the preacher sat to preach, the congregation stood to listen). His *Orations* attracted many to his chapel, winning over significant numbers of Arians and waverers to a belief in the Trinity. Almost any biblical argument for the deity of Christ, and the divine personhood of the Holy Spirit, with which we are familiar today, was probably anticipated by Gregory. I recollect once, many years ago, studying the *Five Theological Orations* on the deity and distinct personhood of the Spirit, when a couple of Jehovah's Witnesses turned up on my doorstep. I found myself immediately reproducing

Gregory's arguments in a sparkling flow of eloquence far from my customary rambling!

By the time the Council of Constantinople met in 381 to give final vindication to the Trinitarian faith against Arianism, Gregory was held in such high esteem by his fellow-Trinitarians that they put him in charge of the Council. It was a bad move. Even amid the triumph of Trinitarian orthodoxy, thorny issues of church politics exploded around the hapless Gregory's head. Increasingly overwhelmed by nervous anxiety, Gregory's confidence collapsed; he resigned from the Council, and went home to Nazianzus. Even here the burden of being its bishop fell upon him, and he found himself embroiled in conflict with local heretics, so-called Apollinarians, whose view of the incarnation was 'a divine mind in a human body,' thus repudiating Christ's full humanity (they denied him a human mind). Gregory could be as blunt with Apollinarians as he had been with Arians: 'Have you placed your hope in a Jesus who was a human being but lacked a human mind? Then you yourself are truly mindless.' After two years of this, Gregory was again weary of life, resigning in 383; he spent his last six years in peaceful retirement.

Gregory left a rich abundance of theological and spiritual literature as a bequest to the church universal. His expositions of the incarnation, exploring and defending the true deity and true humanity of Christ, remain masterful by any standard and by common confession. Likewise his sublime articulations of the mystery of the Holy Trinity:

I set before you the One Deity and Power, found in the Three-in-Unity,
Embracing the Three one by one, equal in essence and nature,
Neither increased nor decreased by ideas of greater or less;
In every way equal, in every way the same,
Just as the loveliness and hugeness of the heavens are one:
The infinite oneness of Three Infinite Ones,
Each of whom is God when seen individually in Himself.
As the Father is God, so is the Son,
And as the Son is God, so is the Holy Spirit;
And the Three are likewise One God when seen together.
Each is God because they are of the same essence,
And they are One God because of the single principle of Deity.
The very instant I conceive of the One,
I am enlightened by the brightness of the Three;
The very instant I differentiate them, I am carried straight back to the One.
When I regard any One of the Three, I think of Him as the Whole;
My sight is filled to the brim,
And the greater part of what I am thinking of eludes me!
I cannot grasp the greatness of One of the Three
So as to reckon a greater greatness to the Others.
And when I see the Three together, I see only one torch,
And I cannot divide or share out the Undivided Light.

(*Oration on Holy Baptism,* ch. 41)

John Calvin quotes from this passage with glowing approval in *Institutes* I:xiii:17. (An Eastern Orthodox scholar once remarked to me, 'Not many realise how steeped Calvin was in the Cappadocian Fathers.')

Gregory shows us that a Christian can leave a bountiful legacy to the church of Christ without having any of the qualities of 'macho' leadership admired in some quarters. This sensitive, nervous, poetically minded man, averse to conflict, easily wounded by the minefields and exhausted by the burdens of public life, has done more to edify thinking Christians in their incarnational and Trinitarian faith than almost any other writer over the past two millennia. 'Gregory the Theologian' seems a very apt title, gladly given by grateful children.

3
Anselm of Canterbury (1033–1109)

> Whoever refuses to believe will not understand. Why? Because whoever refuses to believe will not experience; and whoever will not experience something will have no knowledge of it. Experiencing something is superior to hearing about it. Likewise, the knowledge of someone who experiences something is superior to the understanding of someone who merely hears about it.
>
> (*Epistle on the Incarnation,* ch. 1)

Anselm of Canterbury, along with Bernard of Clairvaux (1090–1153), was one of the few medieval theologians who escaped the most scathing criticisms of the Protestant Reformers. In part, this was owing to Anselm's profound treatise on the atonement, the *Cur deus homo* (see below). In part, it was due to the experiential nature of his understanding of theology, illustrated in the quotation above. Although Anselm often employed reason to speculate in matters theological, and in that sense has been hailed as the 'father of scholastic theology,' he never forgot that the God of Christian belief is One who is known 'experimentally' and intimately by the believing soul. For Anselm, this experimental knowledge of God trumped all intellectual speculations, and even orthodox head-knowledge. As Jonathan Edwards was later to say, in a very Anselmian fashion, he who has tasted honey knows incalculably more about its sweetness than a person who has merely looked at it.

Anselm was born in Aosta, northern Italy, and seemed destined from childhood to be a God-intoxicated man. Raised by a devout mother, he had a famous dream as a child, recorded by his contemporary biographer Eadmer:

> One night during sleep, he felt himself being summoned: he must ascend the mountain and make haste to the Court of God. … The Invisible One, appearing as a King, sat before him, enthroned in splendour. There was no one with Him save His cupbearer, since the rest of the royal household had been dispatched as reapers into the world to gather His harvest. The child entered the court; the Lord summoned him, and he obeyed the summons. Approaching, he sat down at the Lord's feet. With kingly grace and kindness, the Lord asked who he was, where he was from, what he sought. The child answered the questions without fear. Then the King commanded the cupbearer to bring forth some bread and set it before him. The bread was wondrously white; and the child ate the bread in the Lord's presence.

As a young man, Anselm became a monk in the French Benedictine abbey of Le Bec in Normandy, led by the great theologian Lanfranc (1005–89), who later became Archbishop of Canterbury. Anselm was elected Abbot of Le Bec in 1078. In 1093 he followed Lanfranc's footsteps in becoming Archbishop of Canterbury. In England, however, Anselm was involved in prolonged conflict with two English kings, William Rufus (1087–1100) and Henry I (1100–1135), opposing their royal control of church appointments. The conflict was so severe that Anselm spent some years in exile.

Later generations would not remember Anselm for his deeds as Archbishop, but for his writings, which exerted a strong and enduring influence. Philosophers for a thousand years have pondered his 'ontological proof' of God's existence in his *Proslogion*. Anselm seeks to establish God's reality, not on the basis of inferential proofs from the world (such as, that design implies a designer), but rather on the basis of the very concept of God. If only one understands the meaning of 'God,' Anselm argues, one sees that he must necessarily exist. After all, he is by definition the supremely perfect being; but he would hardly be very supreme if he did not actually exist. (This is a crude summary of Anselm's reasoning.) Anselm's argument has waxed and waned in acceptance among philosophers and theologians up to the present day. It has made surprising friends and foes. Thomas Aquinas, the patron saint of those who seek to prove God's existence, rejected it; Karl Barth, one of the most notable enemies of these proofs, accepted a version of it!

More strictly theologically, we have Anselm's epoch-making treatise on the atonement, his *Cur deus homo* (Why the God-Man? Or, Why did God become Man?). It seems astonishing that this was the first systematic-theology work on the nature of the atonement to be written in church history. The first millennium of Christian history was content to have different ideas of the atonement jostling around with each other in the church's collective mind. Anselm at last probes the jostling ideas, to set out a single coherent account. He does it in the form of a theatrical dialogue between Anselm himself and his unfortunately named disciple Boso.

We may summarise Anselm's thesis as follows. Through sin, Man has failed to give God what he owes him (obedience). Now we owe God an atonement for our sin. But sin has a sort of infinite character, having been committed against the God of infinite glory. No human person can offer God an infinite atonement. However, the infinite God can offer it to himself. Therefore, if there is to be atonement, God must become Man, and offer himself—in the person of the infinitely precious God-Man, Jesus Christ—as an infinitely valuable atonement for human sin. This is what has happened in Christ, the incarnate Son who offers himself perfectly to the Father on Man's behalf. As we embrace Christ in penitent faith, his atonement is applied to us, and we are reconciled with God.

The more conservative and Scripture-oriented type of theology in the Western church has tended to follow the thesis of *Cur deus homo* ever since. All shallower ideas of how God and Man are reconciled have been met with Anselm's celebrated retort to Boso's superficial alternatives: 'You have not sufficiently considered the seriousness of sin.'[1]

Anselm was also famous for his written prayers and meditations, which continued to supply food for souls well into the Reformation era. These prayers and meditations place Anselm's ultimate hope as a sinner within the exclusive sphere of God's mercy in Jesus Christ. Typical of his prayers is the following:

> To Thee I have referred all my hope. I have set before Thee my Advocate, Thy beloved Son; Thy glorious Progeny I have placed between Thee and me as a Mediator. I have sent up to Thee, I say, Him as an Intercessor through Whom I trust for pardon. I have sent up in words the Word, Whom I have said to have been sent for my deeds; and I have paid to Thee the Death of Thy most holy Offspring, which I believe to have been endured for me. I believe that the Godhead, sent by Thee, took my Manhood, wherein He deigned to endure bonds, buffetings,

[1] One point in which the Reformers did not follow Anselm was the distinction he made between 'satisfaction' and 'punishment' (a distinction based on medieval legal concepts), and his view that it was satisfaction, not punishment, that Christ offered in our place. However, the Reformers accepted Anselm's basic idea that what Man owes, the God-Man pays on Man's behalf.

> spitting, mockings, yea moreover and to take upon Him the Cross and the nails. This Manhood, first worn with the cries of infancy, wrapped in the mean garments of childhood, harassed with toils, macerated with fastings, worn with watchings, wearied with journeys; afterward beaten with scourges, mangled with punishments, reckoned among the dead, but then dowried with the glory of the resurrection, He hath brought among the joys of Heaven, and set on the Right Hand of Thine exaltation. Lo! this atoneth for me; this atoneth Thee.[2]

John Owen, in his treatise on justification by faith, would later point to such passages in Anselm as a far surer method of consolation for a poor dying sinner than what the Roman Catholic Church in Owen's day offered. Owen was not alone in his positive esteem for Anselm: Thomas Watson, John Flavel, William Cunningham, George Smeaton, R. L. Dabney, and other Reformed divines also regarded Anselm in a fundamentally friendly light, while of course not ignoring his defects.[3]

We might perhaps conclude with a timely word from Anselm on the necessity of a personal communion with God, nurtured by prayer:

[2] Edward Pusey's translation, in his *Meditations and Prayers to the Holy Trinity and Our Lord Jesus Christ by St Anselm* (London: John Henry Parker, 1856), the Second Prayer.

[3] It almost goes without saying that a good theologian does not ignore any perceived defects in another theologian he considers worth studying.

Come along now, little man,
Leave your daily work for a while,
Get away for a while from the swirling storm of your
thoughts.
Put those heavy anxieties to one side,
Free yourself for God for a little while,
And rest for a little while in Him.
Retreat into the innermost room in your soul,
Lock out everything else except God
And whatever can aid you in seeking Him;
And when you have closed the door,
Then seek Him.
Now, my whole heart, say to God,
'I seek Your face;
Lord, it is Your face I am seeking.'[4]

[4] This translation is from *2000 Years of Christ's Power,* vol. 2, pp. 300-1.

4
Theophylact of Ochrid (1050–1109)

> In His humanity, Christ was not Himself liable to the curse, since He fulfilled the Law. But we, who were unable to fulfil the Law, lay guilty beneath its verdict. It was as though an innocent man should choose to die in the place of the guilty condemned to death. Christ, then, embraced the curse of being hanged from a tree, and He thus undid the curse to which we were exposed for our failure to fulfil the Law.
>
> (*Commentary on Galatians*, on ch. 3 verse 13)

Theophylact of Ochrid may be unknown to most of us today—an exotic and perhaps unpronounceable name. However, a previous generation of Reformed thinkers knew him, and looked upon the Greek archbishop as a fountain of wisdom in biblical interpretation. Calvin, Thomas Watson, John Owen, Matthew Henry, John Gill, Charles Hodge, and B. B. Warfield, amongst others, all revered the eleventh-century Eastern scholar, citing his comments in their writings.

Western Christians tend to lose sight of the Eastern Church after the age of the Early Church Fathers. This is a pity, since the East had a rich tradition of theology and spiritual life, which Reformation Protestants often (not always!) found more compatible with their own biblical understanding than what they saw in the Roman Catholicism of their day. Martin Luther, for example, sometimes praised 'the Greek Church' as a repository of excellent Christianity. Luther was no doubt encouraged in his view by the East's longstanding and robust rejection of the Roman papacy along with its doctrine of purgatory and indulgences.[1]

We could call Theophylact 'the Matthew Henry of the Eastern Church.' He wrote a highly prized commentary on the whole of the New Testament, apart from the Book of Revelation, and Old Testament commentaries on Hosea, Jonah, Nahum, and Habakkuk. From its first publication to the present, Theophylact's has been the most widely studied Bible commentary in the Eastern Church in its Greek-speaking lands, and also in much of the Slavic East. The commentary itself is a resourceful blending of previous biblical writings by the Early Church Fathers, particularly

[1] In typically exuberant fashion, Luther once declared, 'The Greeks are not heretics or schismatics, but the most Christian people and the best followers of the gospel on earth.' Not of course that Luther ever became Eastern Orthodox, but the Lutheran tradition did set an example of seeking to establish friendly relations with the Churches of the East. Perhaps surprisingly, the point at which Lutherans stumbled concerning Orthodoxy was not the doctrine of salvation, but the Eastern tradition of venerating icons and the invocation of saints.

John Chrysostom, together with clarifying remarks by Theophylact himself. As noted above, in past days the Reformed community had a lot of respect for Theophylact's commentary, frequently referring to it. Here was a voice from the heart of the Middle Ages that lacked a Roman accent in its prolonged meditation on the Scriptures.

The comparative neglect of Theophylact today probably stems from the simple fact that he wrote in Greek, and most of us, educated though we may be, no longer read Greek as our forefathers did. Calvin, Owen, and Hodge could turn to Theophylact's Greek Bible commentary, and make easy sense of what (for most of us) is a closed book—it's all Greek to us, as they say. Fortunately, some at least of Theophylact's New Testament commentary is now available in English—all four Gospels, Galatians, and Ephesians—expertly translated by the Eastern Orthodox scholar Christopher Stade. This enables us to sample the riches of Theophylact's biblical interpretation for ourselves.

Before following that thought any further, we should perhaps learn a little about Theophylact himself. A Greek-speaking native of the Byzantine Empire,[2] he pursued a glittering vocation that combined the academic and the ecclesiastical. He was personal tutor to the Emperor's son, a deacon in Constantinople's chief church—the Hagia

[2] The Byzantine Empire was the Eastern half of the Roman Empire which, unlike its Western counterpart, did not fall in the fifth century, but continued until the fifteenth century, finally succumbing to the Islamic Ottoman Empire when it captured Constantinople in 1453.

Sophia, one of the world's architectural wonders—and professor of rhetoric in Constantinople's Patriarchal Academy (the first to hold this position). He is remembered, however, as the Archbishop of Ochrid, appointed to that high dignity in 1078.[3] Ochrid was at that time the capital of Bulgaria, a Slavic rather than Greek nation, but within the political embrace of the Byzantine Empire and the spiritual fold of Eastern Orthodoxy.

In many ways, Theophylact did not especially enjoy being Archbishop of Ochrid. He had a deeply ingrained sense of the absolute superiority of Greek over Slavic culture, and could hardly refrain from looking on Bulgars as 'barbarians.' His letters reveal that he endured his new situation as a painful exile from his beloved Byzantine world, perhaps reminding us of Calvin's attitude to Geneva—'I wish God would let me leave this place,' as the Reformer once exclaimed. However, in other ways, Theophylact 'went native' in Bulgaria, outspokenly protesting (for example) on the Bulgars' behalf against what he felt were the excessive taxes imposed by Byzantine officials. How can we expect the Bulgars, he warned Constantinople, to settle down as loyal citizens of the Empire when we treat them so badly? He also extolled the Christian virtues of the Bulgars in his biography of his predecessor, Clement of Ochrid, not a Greek but a Slav.

Theophylact also adopted a refreshingly moderate stance toward Western Catholics (Orthodoxy and Catholicism

[3] Ochrid is variously spelled. Typical variants are Ochrida and Ohrid.

having gone their separate ways in the Great East-West Schism of 1054). He rebuked some of his fellow Orthodox theologians for dishonestly caricaturing Western theology: no truthful criticism of Western error was possible, unless Western theology was rightly understood and fairly represented (a lesson for all apologists). Nonetheless, Theophylact stood firm as a rock in rejecting what he perceived as the real and dangerous errors of Western Catholicism, namely its unbiblical exaltation of the authority of the Roman Pope and its incorrect doctrine of the Trinity.[4]

Turning again to Theophylact's abiding legacy, his New Testament commentary, Reformed readers will (I imagine) be struck by two features in particular. First, Theophylact is perfectly happy with allegorical exegesis, a practice generally frowned on by Protestant commentators. However, we should note that the Archbishop is, on the whole, quite restrained in his use of allegory, and often presents an allegorical understanding of a passage as simply a possible view

[4] East and West parted company over whether, in the inner life of the Trinity, the Holy Spirit proceeds from the Father alone (the Eastern view) or from Father and Son jointly (the Western view). This dispute was bound up with attitudes toward the Nicene Creed, the most cherished creed in Christendom: did the Western Church have the right to alter the original wording of the Creed by adding 'and from the Son' to the Creed's affirmation that the Spirit proceeds from the Father? The West maintained it had the right to add this in order to give fuller and better expression to the doctrine of the Spirit. The East endlessly protested that one portion of the church (the Western) had no right to change a Creed that was the shared property of the whole church. These arguments continue to reverberate to the present day.

held by some commentators. In that sense, we can—if we choose—regard him as a highly valuable reporter of the history of exegesis.

The second feature that might strike us is that Theophylact often, without any apology, expounds justification by faith in a 'Protestant' manner. This comes across notably in his commentary on Galatians. He repeatedly interprets 'justify' as the opposite of 'condemn': in other words, these are legal terms referring to the verdict of a court. This is a far purer theology than the medieval Western mistake which misunderstood 'justify' as effectively 'sanctify.'

Moreover, Theophylact is clear that justification is by faith, not works. In his exegesis of Paul's quotation of Genesis 15:6 in Galatians 3:6 ('Abraham believed God, and it was counted to him for righteousness'), Theophylact interprets the phrase as meaning 'justified by faith.' He sees justification as equivalent to a divine counting, reckoning, or imputing of righteousness to Abraham the believer. He then applies Abraham's status to the New Covenant believer: 'If Abraham, who lived before the day of grace had dawned [*i.e.* before the New Covenant], is justified by faith, it follows that those who are now deemed to be the proper vessels of grace should much more cling to faith.' If justification by faith—being counted righteous through trusting God's promise—applied to Abraham before the New Covenant was established, it applies much more to the New Covenant believer.

To all of which a Reformation Protestant can only say a hearty Amen!

5

John Wycliffe (c. 1330–1384)

> The New Testament is of full authority and open to understanding of simple men, as to the points that be most needful to salvation. The text of Holy Writ be words of everlasting life, and he that keepeth meekness and charity hath the true understanding and perfection of all Holy Writ. It seemeth open heresy to say that the gospel, with its truth and freedom, sufficeth not to salvation of Christian men, without keeping of ceremonies and statutes of sinful men that be made in the time of Satan and Antichrist.
>
> (From Wycliffe's *The Truth of Holy Scripture*)

English Protestants have rightly hailed John Wycliffe as 'the Morning Star of the Reformation.' The proto-Protestant movement he spawned, Lollardy,[1] became a widespread underground 'sect' in Catholic England, of which the

[1] The origin and meaning of the word 'Lollard' is now lost in uncertainty. One theory is that it might mean 'mumbler,' but that merely raises the question why Wycliffe's disciples mumbled!

English Catholic hierarchy lived in permanent dread. When sixteenth-century England began to be affected by the Reformation, Bishop Tunstall of London wrote to Erasmus, 'It is no question of pernicious novelty; it is only that new arms are being added to the great crowd of Wycliffite heresies.'

We are not sure when or where Wycliffe was born, nor even how to spell his name.[2] Much of his career lies buried in obscurity. However, by 1370, he had acquired an international reputation as Oxford University's most celebrated philosopher and theologian. Since Oxford University was one of Europe's greatest intellectual foundations, that says a lot for Wycliffe. It also explains why it was taken so seriously when a man of Wycliffe's stature—the greatest thinker of one of Europe's greatest universities—began criticising the doctrines and practices of the medieval church.

Based on contemporary testimony, historian David Schaff[3] gives a human face to Wycliffe's character and influence:

> Wycliffe was spare, and probably never of robust health, but he was not an ascetic. He was fond of a good meal. In temper he was quick, in mind clear, in moral character unblemished. Towards his enemies he was sharp, but never coarse or ribald. William Thorpe, a young contemporary standing in the court of Archbishop Arundel, bore testimony that 'he was emaciated in body and well-nigh

[2] One German scholar listed thirty ways of spelling the Reformer's surname.

[3] Son of the more famous Philip Schaff, pre-eminent church historian of the nineteenth century.

> destitute of strength, and in conduct most innocent. Very many of the chief men of England conferred with him, loved him dearly, wrote down his sayings and followed his manner of life.'[4]

Wycliffe first became famous as a champion of the English crown and nobility in their struggle with the Roman papacy, as it sought to exercise political control over England. However, his stance was radicalised by the 'Great Schism' of 1378, when two rival Popes were elected—Urban VI and Clement VII—plunging Catholic Europe into crisis. The Schism lasted forty years. The papacy, once seen as the guarantor of Christian unity, was now considered the scandalous cause of disunity. Galvanised, Wycliffe commenced a sustained assault on the entire institution of the papacy and its leading doctrines. His major treatises in this vein were *The Truth of Holy Scripture, On the Church, The Power of the Pope,* and *On the Eucharist.* In these writings, Wycliffe posited Scripture as the only authoritative source of Christian teaching, and a conception of the church as the total body of God's grace-predestined people.[5] Conversely, he rejected the papacy's pretensions to divine authority in the church, and

[4] Vol. 6 of *History of the Christian Church.* Most of the volumes were written by Philip Schaff, but vol. 6 was by his son David, after his father's death. Accessed from the online Christian Classics Ethereal Library, https://www.ccel.org/ccel/schaff/hcc6.html, 6/3/25.

[5] This reveals Wycliffe as a fervent student of the writings of Augustine, great patristic exponent of the doctrine of grace. Wycliffe's (probable) mentor, Oxford theologian Thomas Bradwardine (1290–1349), was also a strong Augustinian.

the late medieval concept of transubstantiation as a wrong understanding of Christ's presence in the Lord's Supper.[6]

Wycliffe's rejection of transubstantiation broke the links binding him to the English establishment. Critiquing the mass was felt as a step too far, and Oxford University expelled the great Reformer and his disciples. Rather than ending Wycliffe's activity, however, his academic exile thrust him into a new stage of reforming, dominated by his translation of the Bible. This he carried out from 1382–84 in the parish church of Lutterworth in Leicestershire.[7] He organised a team of his disciples to translate the Western Church's official Latin Bible (the Vulgate) into English; Wycliffe himself seems to have been responsible for the Gospels. The first of these translations—the first complete English Bible—appeared in 1384; it was a very wooden, literal version of the Vulgate. Wycliffe's secretary John Purvey (1353–1428) produced a second version in 1396, which proved far more widely acceptable (its use of English was more natural and flowing).

At Lutterworth, Wycliffe also trained and sent out preachers, known as the 'Poor Priests.' For Wycliffe, the true heart of Christian ministry lay in the faithful proclamation of the word, rather than in administering the sacraments; it was

[6] Wycliffe's positive understanding of Christ's presence in the Supper was akin to the later Calvinist view of a 'spiritual Real Presence.'

[7] Wycliffe had held the parish priesthood at Lutterworth while teaching at Oxford, but prior to his expulsion from the university he had allowed a curate (a clergyman of lesser rank) to carry out his parish duties for him.

preaching, he argued, that brought about the conversion of sinners and edified believers in the faith. Therefore, if parish priests were not preaching, Wycliffe—like John Wesley in a later day—would seek to make good the deficiency.

We do not know how many Poor Priests there were, nor where exactly they went. Some were academically trained (Oxford graduates), and probably carried copies of the English Bible with them. But it seems likely that others went out equipped only with industrious minds that had memorised the Scriptures, sanctified and devoted hearts, and eloquent tongues that could command a hearing and stir the souls of their listeners. Judging by the subsequent history of Lollardy, they had significant success.

In December 1384, Wycliffe suffered a stroke while conducting worship in the Lutterworth church, dying a few days later. A contemporary Catholic chronicler, Walsingham of St Albans, commented on his death with malevolence:

> On the feast of the passion of St Thomas of Canterbury, John de Wycliffe, that instrument of the devil, that enemy of the Church, that author of confusion to the common people, that image of hypocrites, that idol of heretics, that author of schism, that sower of hatred, that coiner of lies, being struck with the horrible judgment of God, was smitten with palsy and continued to live till St Sylvester's day, on which he breathed out his malicious spirit into the abodes of darkness.[8]

[8] Vol. 6 of Schaff's *History of the Christian Church*. Accessed from the

Wycliffe's body was buried in the Lutterworth church graveyard. In an act of retroactive malice, the authorities dug up his remains some three decades later, burnt them for heresy, and cast the ashes into the nearby river Swift. The words of the seventeenth-century historian Thomas Fuller have immortalised the event:

> They burnt his bones to ashes and cast them into Swift, a neighbouring brook running hard by. Thus the brook hath conveyed his ashes into Avon, Avon into Severn, Severn into the narrow seas, they into the main ocean. And thus the ashes of Wycliffe are the emblems of his doctrine, which now is dispersed the world over.

In so many ways, Wycliffe was a forerunner of the Protestant Reformation:

- He subordinated all other sources of teaching to Scripture as the church's sole ultimate authority.

- He advocated and practised translating Scripture into the native tongue, demanding that all Christians be given the right to read it.

- He exalted biblical preaching as lying at the heart of pastoral ministry.

- He endorsed the marriage of the clergy.

---

online Christian Classics Ethereal Library, https://www.ccel.org/ccel/schaff/hcc6.html, 6/3/25.

• He rejected the medieval view of the sacraments, especially transubstantiation.

• He refuted the papacy's claim to lordship over the church, arguing that Christ alone is the church's head.

• He taught that the church is the entire body of the elect, which cannot be identified with any visible earthly institution.

• Above all, he set forth the free, unconditional, efficacious grace of God as the only wellspring of salvation, a grace that flows to sinners first in eternity through election, and then in time through regeneration, sanctification, and preservation.[9]

Despite persecution, Wycliffe's 'Lollard' movement survived in some strength, and when the Reformation came to England, Lollards were among the first to embrace and promote it. Meanwhile, Wycliffe's theology had taken deep root in Bohemia (today's Czech Republic), whose national Reformer and martyr Jan Hus (1372–1415) was a zealous disciple of the English theologian. The Bohemian 'Hussites' achieved a large degree of independence from the papacy through the Hussite Wars of 1419–34. With the dawn of

[9] He does not, however, seem explicitly to have articulated the Reformation doctrine of forensic justification through faith alone. Some have argued that this was latent in Wycliffe's theology. He does use expressions such as that 'to believe in Christ is life,' and that 'faith is the sum of theology.'

the Reformation, they entered the mainstream of European Protestantism. Strikingly, Martin Luther was a profound admirer of Jan Hus and the Hussites, and thus indirectly of Wycliffe.

Wycliffe deserves his customary title 'Morning Star of the Reformation.' He is an outstanding example in church history, not of what one man can do, but of what God can do through one man.

6

Peter Martyr (1499–1562)

> Our salvation does not depend on us, but on God's choice, by which grace, the Spirit, and faith come to dwell in us. Subsequent to this, the morally commendable life of which Christ speaks becomes a testimony to the world. So, my dearest brothers, I entreat you by the mercy of Jesus Christ to make progress! Let these truths be a ceaseless incentive to your efforts, so that your faith does not stand idle. Translate your faith into practice, so that it will in every way communicate to your fellow human beings the reality of your love.
>
> (*A Plain Exposition of the Twelve Articles of the Christian Faith*, section 29)

Peter Martyr, in his own day, was regarded as a giant among Reformers.[1] John Calvin praised him as 'the best and purest of men'; concerning the right understanding of the Lord's Supper, Calvin judged that Martyr had said the

[1] Peter Martyr Vermigli, to give him his full name. Vermigli is pronounced Vair-mee-lee.

last word: 'The whole matter was given its finishing touches by Peter Martyr, who left nothing further to be desired.' Yet outside scholarly circles, few today have heard of Peter Martyr. The distinguished Methodist scholar Gordon Rupp compared Martyr's systematic theology (the *Commonplaces*) to an extinct dinosaur; Scottish theologian T. F. Torrance called Martyr's demise one of the tragedies of Reformation history. However, a proper estimate of Martyr must rank him as one of the 'founding fathers' of Reformed Christianity, alongside Ulrich Zwingli, Martin Bucer, Heinrich Bullinger, and John Calvin.

Martyr's life story holds an abiding fascination. Hailing from the great Italian Renaissance city of Florence, he became an Augustinian friar in his youth, and lived up to the name of his religious order by immersing himself in Augustine's theology.[2] Between 1530 and 1542 Martyr held a number of leadership positions among Italy's Augustinian friars. Two key events befell him during this time. First, he began reading the writings of the Reformers: Zwingli's *Concerning True and False Religion,* and Martin Bucer's commentaries on the Gospels and the Psalms, made a strong impact on him. Second, he became part of a network of Catholic Reformers owing their inspiration to Spanish humanist Juan de Valdes (1500–41). Valdes' home in Naples had grown into a centre of spiritually-minded renewal of the Catholic Church. These

[2] We recollect that this was same Catholic religious order to which Martin Luther had belonged.

'Catholic Evangelicals,' generally disciples of Augustine and his doctrine of sovereign grace, sought to reform Catholicism from within. Their foremost clerical figure was Cardinal Gasparo Contarini (1483–1542), whose statements on justification by faith were sometimes quoted by Protestants against Rome—'See, your own best men agree with us!'

For a while, Martyr was content to be a Catholic evangelical. Valdes' influence, however, was propelling Martyr ever further towards sheer Protestantism, which he was soon virtually teaching in his Augustinian convent at Lucca in Tuscany (central Italy). At length, this aroused the hostile suspicions of his superiors, who summoned Martyr in the summer of 1542 to appear before the Augustinian governing body, in order to answer for his questionable opinions. Rather than obey this risky summons, Martyr fled from Italy, openly embracing Protestantism.

Martyr's flight took him to the south German city of Strasbourg, the headquarters of Reformed Christianity before Calvin's Geneva assumed that role. Here he taught Old Testament studies, becoming an intimate friend of Strasbourg's pre-eminent Reformer, Martin Bucer (1491–1551). From 1547 to 1553, we find Martyr in the England of King Edward VI, invited by Archbishop Cranmer; he taught theology at Oxford University, a hotbed of Roman Catholic sentiment, and helped to infuse Protestantism into the Anglican Church. When the Roman Catholic Mary Tudor ascended the English throne in 1553, Martyr was placed under house arrest as a dangerous foe of Rome. He might have ended up being burnt at the stake, as so many leading English Protestants were. However, Martyr's Catholic archenemy, Bishop Stephen Gardiner of Winchester, showing his more human side, convinced the queen to allow the Italian Reformer to return unmolested to Continental Europe.

At first, Martyr went back to Strasbourg. But the city that had once been the 'nerve centre' of Reformed Christianity was now controlled by strict and intolerant Lutherans who looked upon the Reformed wing of the Reformation as a massive aberration. Appalled by Lutheran hostility to his faith, Martyr shook Strasbourg's dust off his feet in 1556 and became Professor of Hebrew in Reformed Zurich, at the behest of its illustrious Reformer Heinrich Bullinger (1504–75). His last act of public service to the Reformation was to lead the Protestant deputies—along with Calvin's right-hand man, Theodore Beza (1519–1605)—at the French Colloquy of Poissy in 1561. This conference, sponsored by the French government, was intended to heal the dangerously volatile religious divisions in France between Roman Catholics and Protestants. After hopeful beginnings, the Colloquy collapsed when its proceedings were condemned by the Sorbonne (Paris University's theology faculty, a stronghold of anti-Reformation sentiment). Shortly thereafter, France lurched into the carnage of Catholic–Protestant civil war, lasting for four decades. Martyr had done his best to try to avert this tragic bloodshed.

Peter Martyr's huge impact on his fellow Protestants in the sixteenth and seventeenth centuries came in three ways:

First, Martyr wrote several commentaries on Scripture, which were revered as ideal models of Reformed biblical exposition for the next two hundred years. Most substantial among these was his 1558 commentary on Romans.

Secondly, soon after Martyr's death in 1562, a French Reformed pastor named Robert Masson worked his way through Martyr's biblical commentaries, collecting a vast throng of passages which he organised under topical headings. Entitled *Loci Communes* (or in English, *Commonplaces*), this became a popular Reformed systematic theology for the next hundred years. It was perhaps exceeded only by Calvin's *Institutes* in its influence and renown among Reformed students.

Thirdly, together with Calvin, Martyr fine-tuned the Reformed doctrine of the Lord's Supper into its classical form. We find this in his *Defence of the Ancient and Apostolic Doctrine of the Most Holy Sacrament of the Eucharist* (1559), which was aimed against the Roman Catholic doctrine of the Mass, and his *Dialogue Concerning the Two Natures in Christ* (1561), which engaged with the Lutheran doctrine.[3] The first

[3] Classical Lutheranism held that in the union of the two natures (deity and humanity) in Christ, the divine nature imparted its attributes (such as omnipresence) to the Lord's human nature. This meant that Christ was omnipresent in his humanity, explaining how his body and blood could be present in the bread and wine of the Lord's Supper. Martyr rejected this as an incorrect understanding of how Christ's two natures relate to

of these volumes has been hailed as the greatest single work on the Lord's Supper to have emerged from the controversies of the sixteenth century. Martyr located the Supper strongly within the larger setting of union with Christ, positing that the sacrament was a visible sign through which Christ and his people were bound together in the Holy Spirit. Although the bread and wine were—in their own nature—signs or symbols of Christ's body and blood, the action of the Holy Spirit made them 'instruments,' whereby Christ's body and blood were conveyed to the believer in and through the mysterious power of the Spirit. This is the view of Christ's presence in the Supper that almost all the Reformed creeds and confessions expound. See the Westminster Confession 29:7 for a useful summary statement.

Martyr was more influential than any other Reformed theologian in setting out a distinctively Reformed view of the Lord's Supper and Christ's presence therein, distinguishing carefully between this and the Roman Catholic, Lutheran, and Anabaptist views. The Catholic and Lutheran doctrines he rejected on the ground that Christ's body is located in heaven until the Second Coming, so that it cannot be present in the space occupied by the bread and wine of the Supper, as Catholics and Lutherans held in their different ways. He also rejected the Anabaptist view (which he understood as a bare 'memorialism,' *i.e.* that the purpose of the Supper was

---

each other. It has remained a stumbling block between Lutherans and Reformed Christians ever since.

merely to help believers remember what Christ did). This memorialist view, he argued, neglected the living action of the Holy Spirit, who unites believers to Christ as they share in the Supper, giving us a real life-giving communion in his risen humanity. Martyr also produced a formidable array of support from the Early Church Fathers to undergird the Reformed view; it is doubtful whether anyone among sixteenth-century Protestants excelled Martyr as a student of the Fathers.

Thankfully, many of Peter Martyr's writings have been translated into English in the past few decades, enabling his voice to speak again.[4] It is a voice well worth hearing. The present writer is very glad that he made Martyr's acquaintance as a theology student, and warmly commends the great Italian Reformer as a worthy companion and colleague of Zwingli, Bucer, Bullinger, and Calvin in laying the foundations of our Reformed faith.

[4] Martyr's *Commonplaces*, for example, are currently being translated into modern English through the Davenant Institute. Older translations of Martyr can be found on internet archive sites, but are not necessarily very readable.

7
Francis Turretin (1623–1687)

> Sufferings are of two kinds. In the one, they are exacted by a judge to make satisfaction to justice: in the other, they are inflicted for the correction of the offender. We admit that the latter species of offering is often appointed to believers—not for vengeance, but for healing; not for destruction, but for correction. God lays it upon them, not as a judge, but as a father: not out of hatred, but out of love. Cyprian says, 'The Lord chastises the saints that he may advance their holiness; and he advances their holiness that he may save them.' To the same purpose Thomas [Aquinas] speaks (III. Q. 96): 'Before pardon, the sufferings of the elect are punishments for sin: after pardon, they are exercises.'
>
> (*The Atonement of Christ,* translated by James R. Wilson)

There was a time when Francis Turretin was considered one of the brightest glories of the Reformed Church, a towering theologian with few equals. Jonathan Edwards once praised Turretin in robust terms, as the unchallenged master of all theological controversies:

> Turretin is [excellent] on polemical divinity, on the five points and all other controversial points, and is much larger in these than [other theologians].[1]

Yet Turretin, for all his past glory, was probably not well-known for most of the twentieth century, until the publication of the three volumes of his systematic theology by P&R Publishing in 1992–97. A previous generation had studied Turretin in Latin. With the decline of the knowledge of Latin among academic theologians, and indeed among educated people in general, Turretin's masterwork might have vanished into oblivion.

The illustrious Charles Hodge (1797–1878) of Princeton, however, used Turretin's systematic theology as his textbook for teaching theology to his students. Hodge persuaded his friend, George Musgrave Giger (1822–65), who taught Latin and Greek at Princeton, to translate Turretin into English. This translation was then made available in Princeton's library, in manuscript form, for Hodge's students to consult. It was Giger's translation that was finally published in 1992–97. Suddenly, the Reformed world at large became aware once again of the mighty seventeenth-century theologian who, for two hundred years, had taught their

[1] From a 1746 letter to Joseph Bellamy. Edwards specified Peter Van Mastricht, another great seventeenth-century Reformed theologian, as the one to whom Turretin was superior in matters of theological controversy, although Edwards ultimately preferred Van Mastricht as, overall, a more useful theologian.

forefathers the mysteries, intricacies, distinctives, and biblical grounding of the Reformed faith.

Who, then, was Francis Turretin? And why was his systematic theology once regarded as among the very finest the Reformed world had to offer?

Turretin was born in Geneva to a distinguished Reformed family of Italian origin (their surname was strictly 'Turrettini'). His education took place in an almost bewildering variety of locations and schools of learning—Geneva itself, Leyden, Utrecht, Paris, Saumur, Montauban, and Nîmes. His purpose was to expose his mind to the diversity and fullness of Reformed theology, by experiencing all its educational centres of influence. Among the famous Reformed teachers at whose feet he sat were fellow-Italian Giovanni Diodati (1576–1649), John Milton's friend, who translated the Bible into Italian; the distinguished German theologian Friedrich Spanheim (1600–49); the great Dutch theologian and devotional writer Gisbert Voetius (1589–1676); the controversial Huguenot thinker Moise Amyraut (1596–1664); and Amyraut's internationally renowned scholarly supporter, John Daillé (1594–1670).

Turretin became pastor of the Italian church in Geneva in 1648 (at the age of twenty-five). Although he was by now a naturalised French-Swiss, Turretin still spoke his ancestral Italian fluently. His preaching, according to contemporary testimony, was marked by heartfelt exhortations that his hearers should trust Christ for personal salvation. This alerts us to the fact that the great theologians of post-Calvin Calvinism, although often caricatured as dry 'scholastic' intellectuals, could often be aflame with an authentic experiential piety, head and heart combining in beautiful harmony.

In 1653, Turretin was appointed as Professor of Theology in the Genevan Academy, in succession to his father who had taught at the Academy from 1618 to 1631. Turretin Junior now did the same, but with far greater impact. Hardly anyone now remembers the father; the son's brilliance eclipsed him almost completely.

Turretin's reputation rests on his magnum opus of systematic theology, the *Institutes of Elenctic Theology*. This was published in three volumes, between 1679 and 1685. Over the following fifty years there were six further editions, the last being in 1734. The title may seem obscure. *Elenctic* derives from a Greek word meaning 'to refute.' The elenctic method in logic was also known as the Socratic method, after Socrates, the 'street-philosopher' of ancient pagan Athens, encountering whom was compared with gripping an electric eel. Socrates led people to a clearer knowledge of truth by inviting them to state their beliefs, and then engaging them in dialogue in which he questioned them rigorously. Eventually his dialogue-partners realised that their original statements of belief must have been inadequate or defective, once their inconsistencies and absurdities had been laid bare by Socrates' probing interrogation.

This was precisely Turretin's approach to teaching theology. His *Institutes* did not seek to construct some kind of all-embracing, watertight intellectual system; rather, it investigated a set of disputed issues in the theology of the day. Each particular question stated a controversy between Reformed theology and its critics—Roman Catholics, Lutherans, Arminians, Socinians, and others. Turretin meticulously and fair-mindedly examined alternatives to what he considered the best Reformed view, refuted them to his own satisfaction (and that of most of his readers), and then established the Reformed understanding through biblical exegesis, rational argument, and a subordinate appeal to lesser authorities (*e.g.* the Early Church Fathers).

Turretin's method was identical in substance to the one employed by the great medieval theologian, Thomas Aquinas (1225–74) in his masterwork of systematic theology, the *Summa Theologiae*. Aquinas, indeed, was a strong influence on Turretin in many ways, despite the Reformed Genevan's profound disagreement with some of Aquinas' medieval Catholic distinctives. One significant area where Turretin shared a common mind with Aquinas was in admiring the Greek pagan thinker Aristotle as the best of philosophers. In that sense, Turretin illustrates what has been called the 'Christian Aristotelianism' that generally characterised the great Lutheran and Reformed theologians from the late sixteenth century onwards. The usefulness and appropriateness of this Christian Aristotelianism has been challenged by some Reformed thinkers. Turretin, however, cannot be singled out as unusual in this respect; he was simply following what was regarded as the best method of his day.

At any rate, the result, in Turretin's *Institutes,* is marked by great lucidity and precision. To appreciate the majority Reformed view on virtually any topic in the period of post-Calvin Calvinism, and to see it formulated, expounded, and supported, with a display of limpid reason and breadth of scholarship, there is nothing that excels Turretin. Unsurprisingly, many Reformed seminaries adopted his *Institutes* as the systematic theology of choice. It was so popular that a widely used compendium (an abridged edition) was published by Leonard Rijssen in 1690. In America's shining fortress of Reformed theology, Princeton Seminary in New Jersey, Turretin's *Institutes* was the foundational theological text well into the nineteenth century, until it was supplanted by the *Systematic Theology* of Princeton's own Charles Hodge.

Some of Turretin is surprisingly relevant to present-day controversies. His refutation of Socinianism, for instance, has powerful application to modern evangelical disputes over Open Theism, and that movement's denial of God's foreknowledge of future events, including human choices. This denial was equally characteristic of the Socinians of Turretin's day (the ancestors of what became Unitarianism).

Turretin defended God's comprehensive foreknowledge against Socinianism, providing biblical and philosophical proof of the church's traditional belief in divine foreknowledge. He rejected the Socinian view that God is just as 'imprisoned' within time as we are, and thus can only know things as they actually happen. Rather, Scripture bears witness to God's sovereign transcendence over time: with God, a day is like a thousand years, and a thousand years are like a day (2 Pet. 3:8). Time is God's creation; and as its Creator, God is Lord over time, unconstrained by its creaturely perspectives of yesterday and tomorrow. From a slightly different standpoint, Turretin argued that God knows every event, every human decision—past, present, future—because they all lie within his effectual or permissive decree, through which he governs the universe. Since God knows what he has decided either to cause or permit to take place, the whole history of creation lies open to him.

Again, when many ill-informed evangelicals today are converting to Roman Catholicism, it is good to find in Turretin a masterful exposition of all the main points of contention between Protestantism and Rome, and an in-depth vindication of the Protestant position, drawn both from Scripture and the Early Church Fathers. One can hardly study Turretin on these matters, and then easily convert to Rome.

On the other hand, modern Protestants may need to prepare themselves for what they might think are some potentially surprising things in Turretin. For example, he gives a lengthy and reasoned defence of the patristic title *theotokos*

(God-bearer, sometimes translated 'Mother of God') for Mary the mother of Jesus, and of her perpetual virginity (that Mary remained a lifelong virgin after the Lord's birth). There is little point glossing over such things, since the student of Turretin will soon enough discover them for himself or herself. Many Reformed theologians today still in fact defend *theotokos* as a title for Mary, although very few will now defend her perpetual virginity. However, the latter belief, it should be noted, was defended by Turretin as a 'pious opinion,' not an authoritative dogma.

Turretin's most notable theological contribution to his day was perhaps his opposition to Amyraldianism. This was a version of Reformed theology articulated with great eloquence by Moise Amyraut (1596–1664) in the French Reformed Church. (Amyraut was Latinised as 'Amyraldus.') Its main distinctive was a view of the 'logical order' of God's decrees, which located divine election *after* the atonement, rather than being the motivation *behind* the atonement. For Amyraut and his significant body of followers, God had decreed the atonement as a manifestation of his universal compassion for sinful humanity; then he decreed to elect some to benefit savingly from the atonement, in order that the Saviour's death might have at least some fruit among otherwise sin-enslaved humans. This view was sometimes known as hypothetical or conditional universalism: Christ died for all *on condition* that they believe, and divine election then ensures that some *will* believe. Today, most of us will probably refer to it as 'four point Calvinism' (rejecting 'limited atonement,' the third of the five points of mainstream Reformed soteriology).

After much internal controversy within the French Reformed Church, Amyraldianism prevailed among French Calvinists. Turretin, however, was not convinced that Amyraldianism was as biblical or coherent as the view (which had been more normal among Calvinists) that election logically *preceded* the atonement. In other words, the reason why the Son of God took flesh, and atoned for sin, was precisely because the Trinity had elected some to be saved. Consequently, Turretin resolved to demonstrate the theological mistakes of Amyraldianism, in case any other Reformed church strayed down the path taken by French Calvinists.

Amyraldianism probably never had a more incisive and yet a more fair-minded critic than Turretin. He never denied that Amyraldians were honest Christian men who sought to be authentic Calvinists. However, it may well have been due to Turretin's sustained anti-Amyraldian argumentation, more than any other single factor, that Calvinism outside France preferred to express the doctrine of the atonement in terms of particular redemption.

Should we read Turretin now, in the twenty-first century? The present writer can only give his own considered opinion. I have often consulted Turretin's *Institutes,* and I do not remember ever going away feeling that the exercise had been worthless. Even on those few occasions where I found

I could not follow him, I have found his reasoning to be lucid and a joy to read (not at all a dry exercise in spiritless intellectualism). Certainly the three volumes of his *Institutes* should be on the bookshelf of anyone seriously interested in the history of Reformed theology. They may not be as famous as John Calvin's *Institutes,* but in their own way, and their own day, they were as influential in shaping the minds of generations of Reformed preachers and teachers across the world. They richly repay careful study today.

8

John Wesley (1703–1791)

> I received some blows, lost part of my clothes, and was covered over with dirt: here, although the hands of perhaps some hundreds of people were lifted up to strike or throw, yet they were one and all stopped in the midway; so that not a man touched me with one of his fingers, neither was anything thrown from first to last; so that I had not even a speck of dirt on my clothes. Who can deny that God heareth prayer, or that He hath all power in heaven and earth?
>
> (Wesley's *Journal* for July 4, 1745, describing his evangelism in Falmouth)

John Wesley is well-known as the 'Father of English Methodism.' His abiding impact on world Christianity is undisputed. Had it not been for the epic labours of Wesley and his Methodist co-workers in the eighteenth century, vast swathes of England and the English-speaking peoples would have remained untouched by the gospel.

One of the most absorbing aspects of Wesley's life is his anguished pilgrimage to an assured faith in Christ. He was raised within the High Church Arminian school of Anglicanism, which perceived God's grace as channelled through the Episcopal church order and its sacraments. This was Wesley's outlook when he dominated the 'Holy Club' at Oxford University (the perhaps unlikely seedbed of the Evangelical Revival), and when he went to Savannah, Georgia, to minister in Colonial America. The latter venture proved a failure, leaving Wesley deeply disillusioned with himself. His words on returning to England in early 1738 resonate with a soul-searching honesty that make so much of modern Christianity seem so shallow:

> It is now two years and almost four months since I left my native country in order to teach the Georgian Indians [native Americans] the nature of Christianity—but what have I learned myself in the meantime? Why (what I the last of all suspected), that I, who went to America to convert others, was never myself converted to God. … This, then, have I learned in the ends of the earth: that I am fallen short of the glory of God, that my whole heart is altogether corrupt and abominable, and, consequently, my whole life (seeing that it cannot be that an evil tree should bring forth good fruit) is alienated from the life of God. I am a child of wrath, an heir of Hell. My own works, my own sufferings, and my own righteousness are so far from making any atonement for the least of my

> sins, which are more in number than the hairs of my head, the best of them need atonement, or they cannot abide His righteous judgment. Having the sentence of death in my heart, and having nothing in or of myself to plead, I have no hope but that of being justified freely through the redemption that is in Jesus.

Wesley was brought to saving faith by twin influences radiating from Germany: the Moravian movement and Martin Luther. The Moravians were the descendants of the fifteenth-century Hussites, who in 1727 had experienced remarkable revival, the 'Moravian Pentecost,' under the leadership of Nicholas von Zinzendorf (1700–60), who had given shelter on his land in Saxony to Hussite refugees fleeing from Catholic persecution. Wesley encountered a group of Moravians on the ship that took him out to Georgia, and was astounded by their serene faith in Christ in the face of impending death, as a storm threatened to sink the vessel. Wesley kept up contact with Moravians in Georgia, and on returning to England, virtually put himself under the spiritual guidance of Moravian pastor Peter Boehler (1712–75), fascinated by the Moravian doctrine and experience of assured faith (which he still lacked).

Wesley's conversion was mediated through a Moravian 'Society' meeting in Aldersgate Street, London, in May 1738. (These 'Societies' were associations of believers for mutual edification outside of formal Sunday worship, an integral element in Moravian religious life.) This meeting introduced Wesley to the second German influence in his conversion—Martin Luther. In Wesley's words:

> In the evening I went very unwillingly to a Society in Aldersgate Street, where one was reading Luther's preface to the Epistle to the Romans. About a quarter before nine, while he was describing the change which God works in the heart through faith in Christ, I felt my heart strangely warmed. I felt I did trust in Christ, Christ alone for salvation, and an assurance was given me that He had taken away my sins, even mine, and saved me from the law of sin and death.

Thus occurred the most famous conversion in English religious history. A year later, inspired by the example of his Calvinist friend George Whitefield, Wesley took the momentous step of engaging in open-air preaching at St Philip's Marsh, near Bristol. Wesley proved as effective an open-air preacher as Whitefield, although their styles differed hugely. Whitefield was emotionally intense, dramatic, even theatrical: he would shout, stamp his feet, shed tears, and make up his own conversations with different biblical characters, all in a piercingly loud voice. Wesley by contrast was far more restrained, moderate, and 'factual' in manner, more intent on communicating a clear-cut exposition of biblical truth. But great spiritual power attended his preaching, resulting in abundant professions of faith. Again modelling himself on Whitefield, Wesley became an itinerant preacher, utilising open-air gatherings as a principal method of bringing Christ to the unchurched multitudes. By his own admission, Wesley never actually enjoyed preaching in the open air; still, he humbly gave himself to it as a providential instrument for disseminating the gospel to the masses. He once said:

> I preached to twice the people we should have had at the house [church]. What marvel the devil does not love field-preaching! Neither do I: I love a commodious room, a soft cushion, a handsome pulpit. But where is my zeal, if I do not trample all these under foot in order to save one more soul?

Wesley's almost unparalleled impact was not restricted to his own preaching. He trained a whole generation of Methodist lay preachers who journeyed throughout England, replicating Wesley's message of salvation by faith; some of these men came close to being Wesley's equals in popular influence, *e.g.* the converted stonemason John Nelson (1707–74), whose heroic labours preaching in York, Sheffield, Leeds, and Manchester established thriving bodies of Methodists in those cities.

Further, Wesley organised converts into the Societies he had seen functioning among the Moravians. The formal worship of 'Sunday Christianity' was ineffective, in Wesley's view, for nurturing meaningful faith and sanctification; the Societies gave opportunity for a more personal and authentically communal expression of spiritual life. From 1742, these Societies included the 'class meeting.' This was a smaller, more intimate body of between ten and twelve people, drawn from a variety of backgrounds (age, social occupation, length of time a person had been a convert). It met on a weekly basis with the aim of deepening the faith and spiritual life of members. This purpose was carried out through members reporting to the meeting on how their sanctification was progressing. Such personal (often intimate) reports fostered openness about the realities of Christian experience. Wesley drew up a set of rules to guide the practical conduct of all class members, who were interviewed on a regular basis to make sure that they were keeping to these rules.

Wesley's organisational genius shaped the Methodist movement into one of the most triumphant expressions of faith in the Christian history of England. By the time of Wesley's death in 1791, his Societies had a listed 71,688 members and 294 preachers in Britain, and 43,265 members and 198 preachers in America. These figures tell their own story, especially given relatively small population levels in the eighteenth century, and the deeply committed nature of Society membership.

Of course, there remains the question of Wesley's Arminianism; but a cautionary note should perhaps be sounded. Wesley's brand of Arminianism was far removed from the prevailing type of Arminianism too often encountered today. The chief difference is found in Wesley's belief in total depravity. By nature, he held, the human will lies in a bondage to sin as grim and devastating as Augustine, Luther, and Calvin had ever taught. Contrast this with today's 'popular Arminianism' (as we might call it) which teaches that man's will is by nature free—a position more akin to the Pelagian heresy combatted by Augustine.

What separated Wesley from Augustine, Luther, and Calvin was his belief that human nature's total depravity has been offset by a universal gift of grace, flowing from the work of Christ, which enables people to respond positively to the Holy Spirit—sufficient or prevenient grace, in Wesleyan parlance. This differs from Augustine, Luther, and Calvin's conviction that divine grace does not merely enable, but efficaciously produces, man's positive response to the gospel. Even so, it seems only right and truthful to recognise how much closer Wesley stood to Reformation teaching on this topic, in contrast with the modern Arminian exaltation of man's will as inherently free.

It might be useful to close with an anecdote credited to George Whitefield, who was once asked by a narrow-minded fellow Calvinist 'whether we shall see Mr Wesley in heaven.' Whitefield replied, 'No, we shall not see him; for he shall be so close to the Throne, and we so far away, that we will not be able to see him.' A truly sovereign God need not limit himself to working through those with a fully correct understanding of his sovereignty.[1]

[1] Much of this account is distilled from a far longer and more detailed assessment of John Wesley in vol. 5 of *2000 Years of Christ's Power*, ch. 2.

9

Jonathan Edwards (1703–1758)

> A great and earnest concern about the great things of religion and the eternal world, became universal in all parts of the town, and among persons of all degrees, and all ages. The noise amongst the dry bones waxed louder and louder; all other talk but about spiritual and eternal things, was soon thrown by; all the conversation, in all companies and upon all occasions, was upon these things only, unless so much as was necessary for people carrying on their ordinary secular business. Other discourse than of the things of religion would scarcely be tolerated in any company.
>
> (Edwards on the revival in Northampton, New Hampshire, described in his *Faithful Narrative of the Surprising Work of God.*)

Jonathan Edwards is by common consent America's greatest theologian, whose writings impacted generations to come. He is rightly situated within the Reformed tradition; this, however, should not blind us to his massive independence of mind, which occasionally took him in directions where most Reformed thinkers have not been willing to travel (see below).

Edwards was born in New England, at East Windsor in the Colony of Connecticut, son of Congregationalist pastor Timothy Edwards. A childhood genius, Edwards Junior studied theology at Yale College, where he became a tutor in 1724, until finally taking up the position for which he is known in 1727—associate pastor with his grandfather Solomon Stoddard at the Northampton Congregationalist Church in the Colony of Massachusetts. After Stoddard's death, Edwards became the church's sole pastor.

In the period 1734–35, revival swept through Northampton, described in vivid detail in Edwards' *Faithful Narrative of the Surprising Work of God in the Conversion of Many Hundred Souls in Northampton* (1737). The first of Edwards' writings to be widely circulated, it was studied with great interest by British evangelicals—Isaac Watts, John Wesley, Howell Harris, and others, helping to instil the idea of revival in their minds. Northampton's revival resulted in three hundred of the town's young adults being received into membership in Edwards' church. The movement spilled out from Northampton across the Connecticut River valley, becoming an integral ingredient in America's 'Great Awakening.' The fire of revival eventually died down in Northampton, but beginning in September 1740, an even more profound spiritual movement was triggered by George Whitefield's preaching in Boston, Massachusetts, and its environs. This was followed by Whitefield's preaching tour through Connecticut, where Whitefield and Edwards became firm friends.

If Whitefield was the foremost preacher of America's Great Awakening, Edwards became its foremost theologian. Arguably his greatest theological masterworks were those treatises in which he wrote as a pastoral and experiential thinker, exploring the nature of true spiritual experience, and discerning its harmful counterfeits. His most prominent works in this style were his *Distinguishing Marks of a Work of the Spirit of God* (1741), *Thoughts Concerning the Present Revival in New England* (1743), and *Treatise Concerning Religious Affections* (1746).

In these writings, Edwards navigated a *via media* between a dead and dusty orthodoxy on the one hand, and a false and unhinged emotionalism on the other. He counselled that mere emotionalism would always be present in revivals, giving those imprisoned within a 'high and dry' orthodoxy an excuse to reject all revivals as mindless frenzy. For Edwards, however, Scripture gave sufficient criteria to differentiate between the wholesome wheat of the Holy Spirit and the chaff of false human emotions, or Satan's deceptions, in any apparent work of grace.

When Edwards turned from experiential to doctrinal theology, his masterworks were his *A Careful and Strict Inquiry into the Modern Prevailing Notions of the Freedom of the Will* (1754) and *The Great Christian Doctrine of Original*

Sin Defended (1758). In these treatises, he expounded a fundamentally Augustinian/Reformed perspective on human sin and divine grace. A good deal of Edwards' theology here was hammered out in response to the radically Arminian English theologian Daniel Whitby (1638–1726). Whitby felt a tension, even an inconsistency, between God's eternal foreknowledge of all future events and any significant freedom for human beings. If all human choices are infallibly foreknown by God, how can we choose anything other than what God has foreknown? Does divine foreknowledge not effectively dictate what humans will choose? In view of this apparent problem, Whitby argued that the safer course was to deny God's foreknowledge rather than the liberty of the human will, in order to safeguard human responsibility and God's non-authorship of sin.

Edwards responded to Whitby's radical Arminianism by positing that humans could possess genuine freedom as long as they were free to act in accordance with their strongest motive. This involved a form of 'determinism' (every choice flows inevitably from the strongest motive), which meshed very comfortably with Edwards' belief in God's perfect foreknowledge and sovereign control over all the choices and actions of his creatures. For Edwards, humans enjoy a meaningful freedom, if we are free to act on our own strongest motive without being subject to outward compulsion.[1]

[1] It should be noted that not all Reformed thinkers have held a determinist view of the human will. The illustrious Scottish Calvinist of the

A few areas where Edwards' theology has not generally been followed by mainstream Reformed thinking include his view of creation as 'continuous creation' (crudely that God continually re-creates everything moment by moment), his rather philosophical and arguably speculative doctrine of the Trinity, and his suggestion that perfect repentance—if only it could be offered—would be a sufficient atonement for sin.[2] However, in these as in other areas, lively debate about Edwards' meaning is ongoing among scholars. There are enough different schools of 'Edwards interpretation' to caution us against easy judgments.

Edwards' most well-known sermon, *Sinners in the Hands of an Angry God,* has exposed him to much criticism; sometimes it is the only specimen of Edwards' writing reprinted in collections of eighteenth-century American literature,

nineteenth century, John 'Rabbi' Duncan, criticised Edwards' determinism because it could not be true of humankind prior to the Fall. If all choices are determined by the strongest motive, it must follow that Adam sinned because his 'strongest motive' was to disobey God. But in that case, Adam's nature must already have been sinful. However, God created Adam innocent and holy. The great nineteenth-century Southern Presbyterian theologian John L. Girardeau made similar criticisms of Edwards. William Cunningham, another nineteenth-century Scottish Calvinist, usefully distinguished between theological Calvinism and philosophical determinism in his essay *Calvinism and the Doctrine of Philosophical Necessity*.

[2] The Scottish theologian John Macleod Campbell (1800–72) was to make Edwards' view of 'perfect repentance as sufficient atonement' the basis of his epochal treatise *The Nature of the Atonement* (1856), which rejected penal substitution and presented Christ as enacting a perfect representative repentance on our behalf.

giving the impression that it was typical of his preaching and theology. The sermon was originally preached at Enfield, Connecticut, in 1741. But it would be wrong to think that this sermon sums up Edwards. The beauty of Christ and his perfections, rather than God's wrath, sit at the heart of Edwards' teaching, and the theme of divine anger does not occupy a particularly prominent place in his theology generally. If one attribute of God should be regarded as typifying Edwards' teaching, it is the divine beauty; he was *par excellence* the Theologian of Beauty, not the Theologian of Wrath. Edwards' theology found its 'central dogma' in God's beauty or loveliness. For Edwards, this beauty constituted God's pre-eminent attribute (the 'beauty of holiness'), which he argued was manifested above all in Christ. Edwards' apologetics were rooted in the divine loveliness: the Holy Spirit gave a new faculty of vision to the believer to see the unique and matchless beauty of Christ and his gospel, which was sufficient in itself to produce a deep conviction of the gospel's divine origin and truth.

Despite Edwards' greatness as a theologian, his popularity among his own people in Northampton waned, resulting in his dismissal from the pastorate in 1750.[3] He now went as a missionary to Stockbridge in Massachusetts, where he preached both to white colonists and the Native Americans

[3] The final issue that brought about his dismissal was his attempt to restrict admission to the Lord's Supper to those who credibly professed personal faith, which was contrary to the New England tradition.

of the Housatonic valley. In January 1758, he accepted the position of President of New Jersey College at Princeton (which explains why, in the older literature, he is often called 'President Edwards'). Still, he was not destined to hold the presidency of New Jersey College for very long. Smallpox ravaged the locality in 1757–58, and Edwards submitted to variolation, an early form of inoculation. As a committed advocate of what was then 'modern' science, Edwards was very much in favour of inoculations. The science of vaccination was, however, then in its primitive stages; the procedure of variolation against smallpox carried with it a small chance of dying. Edwards had never been blessed with strong health, and he died on 22 March 1758, at the age of fifty-four, owing to an adverse reaction to the inoculation. His legacy abides in a vast collection of some of the most stimulating writings ever penned by a Reformed theologian.

10

Tikhon of Zadonsk (1724–1783)

The gospel, from its very name, is the happiest of news. To all the world, it proclaims Christ the world's Saviour, who came to seek out the lost and save them. Listen, then, all you lost sinners! Listen to that extremely sweet voice of the gospel! It loudly declares to us all, 'The Son of Man has come to seek and save what is lost.' It is a dreadful thing for us to be found in a state of sin in God's sight. But the gospel proclaims that our sins are forgiven on account of Christ's name, and that Christ is our justification in God's sight. In You, O my Saviour, Jesus Christ, God's Son, I am justified! You are my truth, You are my illumination!

(*Journey to Heaven, Part II: The Way of Salvation*)

One of the happy surprises of church history is finding a new friend, even a hero of the faith, in unforeseen places. When I began researching and writing volume 5 in the series *2000 Years of Christ's Power,* I knew it would be on the eighteenth century. And perhaps I thought that any experience of heart-speaking-to-heart, across the gulf of three hundred years, would be between myself and (say) George Whitefield, Jonathan Edwards, or Andrew Fuller. To my surprise, however, I also found my heart drawn to a man rather unknown in the Protestant West today: a Russian monk by the name of Tikhon. He was a kind of lovable curmudgeon. One cannot help sniggering at some of Tikhon's attitudes—pretending to be ill when he could not face yet another pilgrimage from those tiresome Russian ladies who sought his blessing. 'Tell them I have a sore throat, Ivan. I am not seeing them today. Get one of the other monks to bless them. Ah! Peace at last.'

However, by any Christian standard, Tikhon was a spiritual giant. I had stumbled across him before, back in the 1990s. This was when one of Tikhon's devotional masterpieces was translated into English as *Journey to Heaven*. I bought a copy, dipped into it, and was struck by its directness, its deeply personal grasp of eternal realities, and its spiritual vibrancy. This, I thought, could have been written by a Puritan.

It would be fair and accurate to describe Tikhon of Zadonsk as one of the most influential devotional writers in the entire history of Eastern Orthodoxy. He so impressed and captivated the great Russian novelist Dostoevsky that he made Tikhon a character in two of his novels (*The Brothers Karamazov* and *The Possessed*), stating: 'I will not be creating something from nothing, but simply revealing the real

Tikhon, whom I fervently embraced in my heart a long time ago.' Tikhon has been almost equally fascinating to Protestant scholars. This is because Tikhon himself was a humble disciple of the pre-eminent Lutheran devotional writer Johann Arndt (1555–1621), the 'father of Pietism,' whose epochal treatise *True Christianity* became Tikhon's favourite reading after the Bible. As Tikhon once advised a young Russian noble: 'Always, morning and night, study the Bible and Arndt; you should only skim other books.'

Tikhon was born in Korotsko, in the area of western Russia dominated by the city of Novgorod. His early life as a seminary tutor and bishop is interesting in itself, but he found his true calling, and paradoxically his fame, only when he forsook this more public life to become a monk in the Zadonsk monastery, near the River Don, about two hundred and forty miles south of Moscow. Tikhon endeavoured to practise a solitary life at Zadonsk, secluding himself in a monk's cell, and never joining the other monks for meals at the common table in the refectory. But he had a few devoted friends among the monks of Zadonsk, especially the elderly Theophanes, with whom he almost always took his meals, and Tikhon's cell-attendants Chebotarev and Ivan Yefimov, who both wrote biographers of their master. Still, Tikhon avoided contact with most people, feeling a special aversion to the wealthy and the Russian nobility; he found them spiritually shallow, Christians in name alone. His biographer Yefimov recorded:

> He used to take note of the members of the upper classes who were visiting the monastery as pilgrims: the ladies dressed up in flamboyant finery, parading around flirtatiously, their faces plastered with paint and powder. Seeing this, his Grace would say, 'Alas for these poverty-stricken, blind "Christians"! They decorate their perishing bodies, but hardly bother to adorn their souls. Their souls are as spiritually dark as the skin of a Moroccan Muslim who has no knowledge of God and no faith in Jesus Christ our Lord.' When some of these dolled-up ladies sought his blessing, if he had no personal acquaintance with them, he used to decline them admittance into his cell, claiming that he was unwell. At other times he would send them away, through me, to be blessed by the monastery's priest-monks.

Tikhon felt comfortable only with children, unschooled peasants, the poor, and criminals (whom he would often visit in prison). When he left his cell and travelled outside the monastery, he often sang the psalms, having memorised them all.

Tikhon's cell-attendant Yefimov, in his biography of his master, made much of the extraordinary spiritual experiences that seemed to encompass Tikhon like a cloud—visions, heavenly dreams, and so forth. Others noticed that Tikhon's face was often wet with copious tears, an outward sign of his deep sense of sin (this was not something entirely peculiar in the Eastern tradition, which valued the 'grace of tears' as a special gift of the Spirit). When other monks ridiculed Tikhon for his simple and God-focused lifestyle, Yefimov and Chebotarev heard him respond with, 'It is the will of God that—on account of my sins—the brethren should laugh at me. But I do not follow the path of revenge. Forgiveness is better than revenge.'

Tikhon's huge spiritual influence on the Eastern Church came through his devotional writings. The pinnacle of his literary activity in his cell was his six-volume *True Christianity* (1776), named after Johann Arndt's Pietist treatise. This was Tikhon's masterwork. We can understand it as an adaptation to an Eastern context of Arndt's Lutheran meditations on what constituted genuine piety. The central theme in Arndt and Tikhon is virtually identical: a critique of mere 'churchianity' (religious nominalism), and the need for a personal, experiential faith, issuing in a life of ongoing sanctification. Tikhon set forth these concerns with striking effect. In the words of the outstanding twentieth-century Orthodox theologian, Georges Florovsky (1893–1979),[1] Tikhon had a gift of writing with crystal lucidity, allied to a vivid sense of journeying as a pilgrim through this present life, rather than being its inhabitant. At any rate, *True Christianity* was a popular best-seller; many Orthodox seminaries adopted it as a textbook, and it was read with enthusiasm by serious-minded Orthodox people across the whole of Russia.

[1] Georges is correct—not George.

Coupled with his theme of a vital life-transforming faith, Tikhon fully echoed Arndt's Lutheran views on justification by such faith alone:

> It is impossible to become justified before God, and thus saved, without Christ and outside Christ, but only by faith in Christ. The sinner is like a little child standing naked before his mother, asking for clothing, and receiving as a garment the clothes of justification, namely, the righteousness of Christ, which he receives by faith.

Tikhon's other notable works on practical, experiential Christianity included his *A Spiritual Treasure Collected from the World* (1770), adapted from a seventeenth-century treatise by the great Anglican Calvinist Joseph Hall (1574–1656), Bishop of Exeter: another example of Tikhon's willingness to place a positive estimate on anything he judged good in Western Christian literature. After Tikhon's death, Russia's Holy Synod edited an extremely popular anthology of his writings under the title *Counsels on the Particular Duties of Every Christian.*

Tikhon's devotion to the Bible is also worth noting. He once gave this exhortation:

> Take delight in the word of God, I mean the Scriptures that have been handed down to us by the prophets and apostles, even as you would take delight in God Himself. For God's word is the very word of God's own mouth. If you take delight in God, then for certain you will also

> take delight in the word of God. For God's word is God's epistle or letter to us, unworthy though we are, and is His superlative gift to us to bring us salvation. If you take delight in the Sender, then make sure you also take delight in the letter He has sent to you. For God's word is given by God to me, to you, and to everyone, so that all who wish to be saved can receive salvation through it. You rejoice when an earthly king writes a letter to you; you read his letter with delight and joy. How much more should we read the Heavenly King's letter with delight and joy!

Three years before Tikhon's death in 1783, he had been praying intently, 'Tell me, Lord, of my end.' He then had a dream in which he was standing close to a vast, beautiful field, on whose ground there stood wondrous palaces. He longed to enter the field, but an angel told him, 'You will be allowed to enter in three years' time. For the time being, though, carry on with your labours.' The dream impacted Tikhon so deeply, his reaction was to seclude himself even more resolutely in his monk's cell. He was a relatively young fifty-nine when he died.

For the next one hundred and fifty years, Tikhon was the most widely read and best-loved spiritual writer throughout the length and breadth of the Russian Empire. The Russian Church declared him a saint in 1861. His works were frequently republished, resulting in an ever-flowing stream of new readers and disciples. Even today his influence lives on, and has now spread to English-speakers, through the translation of his *Counsels on the Particular Duties of Every Christian* into English in 1991 as *Journey to Heaven*. He embodies an astonishing confluence of Orthodox and Lutheran piety that has edified untold millions.[2]

[2] This chapter condenses a much fuller account of Tikhon given in vol. 5 of *2000 Years of Christ's Power*, ch. 7, section 2.

II

Benjamin Breckenridge Warfield (1851–1921)

> Plato supposed that if ever a divine man should come into the world, men would assuredly crucify Him. And an observant modern novelist remarks that 'there is certainly a "tyrannous hate" in the world for unusual goodness, which is a rebuke to it.' But no man ever so feels his utter depravity as when he thinks of himself as standing by the side of Jesus. In this presence, even what we had haply looked upon as our virtues hide their faces in shame, and cry, 'Depart from us, for we are sinful men, O Lord.'
>
> ('Jesus the Measure of Men,'
> in *The Presbyterian Messenger*, January 18, 1894)

B. B. Warfield of Princeton is usually regarded as the great exponent of the doctrine of biblical inerrancy. He was indeed this, for the modern church; but we must add an immediate note of caution, for fear of misrepresenting the matter. The problem is that many critics of inerrancy like to paint Warfield as the virtual inventor of the doctrine, in order to fix upon it the charge of unhistorical novelty.

Demonstrably, however, Warfield was not crafting a novelty; the doctrine of biblical inerrancy (that the text of Holy Scripture, as it proceeded from prophets and apostles, is true and trustworthy in everything it teaches) has an ancient pedigree, stretching back to the Early Church Fathers. Before we go any further, it is worth fixing that point in our minds. Warfield was employing his eminent intellectual gifts to 'repackage' (to use the word), for the post-Enlightenment church, a belief found lucidly enough in Augustine. To quote the great North African Father:

> I believe strongly concerning these writings alone [the biblical writings] that none of their writers made mistakes in what they wrote. If I am baffled by anything in these writings, seeing something that seems to me contrary to the truth, then without hesitation I assume that either the manuscript is defective, or else the translator did not succeed in capturing the meaning of what was said, or I myself have failed to understand it (Epistle 82:3 to Jerome).

Warfield was setting forth this ancient conviction of the church in a modern setting, as many professing Christians (evangelicals among them) were abandoning the doctrine in the face of 'critical' approaches to Scripture.

Let us, however, turn to the man himself. Warfield was a Virginian by ancestry; his parents were wealthy Virginians who had moved to Kentucky, where Warfield was born, near Lexington, in 1851. This means that he lived through the American Civil War in his childhood; one of his uncles, John C. Breckenridge, was a general in the Confederate army during that conflict. To the end of his days, Warfield reflected his Southern origins; as one contemporary said, 'There was something remarkable in his voice. It had the liquid softness of the South, rather than the metallic resonance which we look for in those who breathe the crisp air of a Northern climate.'[1]

Warfield's decision as a young man to study theology surprised everyone. He had, prior to this, been a devotee of science and mathematics. After an academically distinguished period of study at Princeton Seminary in 1873–76—where Reformed theology, embodied in the Seminary's famous principal Charles Hodge (1797–1878), still pursued a resplendent course—Warfield travelled to Germany with his recently married wife Annie, to continue his studies. Tragically, the young couple were caught in a shattering thunderstorm while walking in the Harz mountains; Annie suffered a nervous breakdown from which she never recovered, and Warfield spent the rest of his life caring for her. (We often forget such anguished human details when reading the works of theologians and devotional authors.)

After a brief pastorate in First Presbyterian Church, Baltimore (1877–78), Warfield became New Testament

[1] After the Civil War, Warfield was a strong opponent of racial segregation and religious discrimination against the newly free black people of the South.

Professor at Western Theological Seminary in Allegheny (now Pittsburgh Theological Seminary). He moved in 1887 to Princeton, where he taught for the rest of his life as Professor of Polemic and Didactic Theology, dying in 1921. History remembers him as the last great representative of Old Princeton theology, combining an orthodox Reformed faith with intellectual brilliance and massive erudition.

Warfield's rich and vigorous exposition of the verbal inspiration and inerrancy of Scripture remains standard even today. His understanding of these doctrines was complex, requiring and repaying close attention on the reader's part. One area where he laid particular emphasis was the nature of divine inspiration. The Holy Spirit, Warfield insists, so interacted with the human authors of Scripture that he fully preserved and utilized their own personalities, and individual forms of literary expression, in the production of the written word. This explained the different and distinctive styles of the biblical writers, and the sense of their own personalities that pervades their compositions. Warfield was seeking to guard against a 'mechanical' view of inspiration that reduced the human authors of Scripture to mere mindless automata in the hand of God. There was, instead, a mysterious 'concurrence' between divine and human authors that allowed the latter to act as genuine free agents, while ensuring that the written product was precisely what the Spirit intended them to say, thereby to convey His message to mankind.

Warfield's studies of Reformed soteriology led him to the celebrated conclusion that a Reformed understanding of human salvation was simply religion itself in its purest form. Religion has to do with Man's relation to, and dependence upon, God. That relational dependence, Warfield argues, is nowhere more fully expressed than in the 'monergism' of the Augustinian/Reformed view of salvation, wherein everything good (and everything of salvific value) in Redeemed Man must be ascribed to the pure, creative grace of God. To the degree that other soteriologies fall short of this, they are failing to express authentic religion, and sliding into a man-centredness that is true religion's rival and opposite.

Warfield was a deservedly renowned apologist for the truth-claims of Christianity. He saw, and wished everyone to see, no contradiction between the faith once delivered to the saints and the life of the intellect. The most thoughtful person could (and should) be a humble Christian, and every Christian could (and should) be a thoughtful person according to their capacity. It is the unbeliever, Warfield argues, who time and again will be shown to be resting on faulty assumptions in his own outlook and his grasp of what Christians believe. When modern secular thought tends to scorn the Christian faith as obviously false and absurd, Warfield's robust intellectual confidence in the truth of the faith, communicated in multiple volumes of genius-level essays and articles, is intensely vital and refreshing.

Warfield's conviction about faith and intellectual life, coupled with his early zeal for science, led him to take a somewhat conciliatory approach to the theory of evolution. The exact character and extent of this conciliatoriness is a matter of ongoing debate. In general, we can say that Warfield did not think there was anything in Scripture that ruled out an evolutionary account of life's development; he wanted instead to discuss the theory in strictly scientific terms. If it could be shown to be bad science, Warfield would dismiss it, and he often voiced scepticism about a variety of scientific arguments for evolution.

Many Reformed believers, of course, think that Darwin's theory runs against the actual teaching of Scripture. It may be worth remembering that Warfield's great Princeton predecessor, Charles Hodge, took this negative Scripture-based view of the Darwinian account of evolution, resting as it did on a notion of 'chance' or 'random' change in the adaptability of life-forms. Hodge rejected this precisely on *biblical* grounds: there can be nothing 'chance' or 'random' in a universe created and governed by a sovereign God. Hence Hodge's famous conclusion: 'What is Darwinism? It is atheism.'

We might have preferred it had Warfield followed more simply in Hodge's footsteps here; but we can at least salute his fair-minded and consistent endeavour to wrestle with the scientific basis and the proposed evidence for evolution on their own terms. Certainly there are no studies of Darwin and religion that have excelled Warfield's, in which he painfully traces the decay of Darwin's religious sentiments under the impact of his own theory (in 'Darwin's Arguments against Christianity and against Religion'). And Warfield complained bitterly that even in his own day, many were erecting evolution into an all-embracing pseudo-science that excluded the supernatural:

> Over against the Christian conception there has arisen in our day, however, a movement which has undertaken to explain the world and all that it contains without God, without any reference to any unseen, supernatural, spiritual element. The watchword of this movement is 'evolution.' And its confession of faith runs, 'I believe in an eternal flux and the production of all things out of their precedent conditions through the natural inter-workings of the forces intrinsic to the changing material.'

The treasure-trove of Warfield's writings shows us one of the finest intellects that ever lived, expounding the many-sided truths of biblical Christianity with profound scholarship and in crystalline prose. When (if I may so put it) I have nothing better to do on a Sunday afternoon, I know I can use my time to excellent effect in picking up and perusing a volume of Warfield, whether on the Divine Messiah of Old Testament prophecy, the emotional life of Jesus, or any of a hundred other topics. The world of believing theology would be so much the poorer without him.

12

J. Gresham Machen (1881–1937)

> Liberalism on the one hand, and the religion of the historic church on the other, are not two varieties of the same religion, but two distinct religions proceeding from altogether separate roots.
>
> (*Christianity and Liberalism*)

John Gresham Machen[1] was the man in whom the tensions between traditional credal Christianity and the forces of liberalising modernism broke into the open in titanic conflict. He looms larger in the American consciousness than elsewhere; but this is not to deny that his influence has been felt in other lands. One of my closest English friends was delivered from liberalism and converted to biblical faith by reading Machen's classic *Christianity and Liberalism*.

[1] There are various ways of pronouncing 'Gresham' and 'Machen,' but in our subject's case, Gresham was pronounced 'Gressum' and Machen was pronounced 'May-chun.' Confusingly for devotees of supernatural fiction, the great Christian fantasy writer Arthur Machen (no relation, though he lived at the same time) pronounced his own name 'Macken.'

Machen was a native of Baltimore, Maryland, born on 28 July 1881. Like his great mentor B. B. Warfield, he was a Southerner by heritage and conviction; part of this heritage included membership in the Southern Presbyterian Church. Machen's father was a brilliant and wealthy lawyer, and Machen grew up at the very heart of cultured Maryland society.

Machen studied classics (Greek and Latin language and literature) at Johns Hopkins University, followed by theology at Princeton Seminary, where he sat at the feet of orthodox giants like Warfield and Francis Patton (1843–1932). After Princeton, he spent a year studying in Germany, in 1905. Here his life was shaken to the core by the leading liberal theologian Wilhelm Hermann (1846–1922) of Marburg University, whose joyous passion in communicating Christ—as Hermann understood him—overwhelmed Machen. Hermann belonged to the then dominant Ritschlian[2] school of German liberalism, which conceived of Jesus in terms of his practical religious 'value,' and the moral impact he makes on those who encounter him through the New Testament and its proclamation. Jesus, for Hermann, was not God incarnate as classically understood, but possessed all the *value* of God for the human soul; he was the one object in the world that awakened and inspired 'absolute confidence and an absolute joyful subjection; [so] that through Jesus we come into communion with the living God and

[2] After Albrecht Ritschl (1822–89), founder of the school.

are made free from the world' (Machen's summary of Hermann's teaching).

We may wonder why Machen was so overpowered by Hermann. Part, at least, of the answer seems to be that he discovered, in Hermann, a passionate and sincere devotion to Christ, bubbling over with life and joy, that he had not (as yet) found in biblical Christianity as represented by its contemporary teachers. When orthodoxy is dull and grey, if not quite dead, it inflicts upon itself a catastrophic wound, tempting honest souls to seek life and joy elsewhere. Machen was 'almost persuaded' by Hermann to become a Ritschlian liberal.

Ultimately, Machen stood firm in his Reformed faith, unwilling to trade in his belief in the Redeemer's true deity, no matter how clothed such denials were in passion, devotion, sincerity, and cutting-edge scholarship. But he had trembled on the brink. This meant that his coming conflict with liberalism would be no detached matter; Machen had seen the face of the enemy at its most beautiful and seductive, and nearly surrendered. This enabled him to contend with liberalism as one who had felt its warm embraces, so that he grasped the nature of the conflict, as it were, from within.

In 1906, Machen began his teaching career at Princeton Seminary, with New Testament as his subject. His time at Princeton coincided with the great Fundamentalist-Modernist controversy in American Christianity.

'Fundamentalist' was derived from a twelve-volume essay series, *The Fundamentals: A Testimony to the Truth* (1910–15). The term is now pejorative, denoting a narrow-minded obscurantism, perhaps allied to religious intolerance and even violence. That, however, would be an unfair and inaccurate characterisation of the original movement, which overflowed with scholarship and mental breadth, counting among its proponents such luminaries as Warfield himself and Scottish Reformed giant James Orr (1844–1913).

As the Fundamentalist movement developed, it is true that it began taking on some of the less attractive qualities for which it later became notorious. Machen himself was always ambivalent about the name and the movement, despite coming to be regarded as its prime champion; he disliked its growing preoccupation with what he felt were cultural taboos rather than clear biblical essentials, and absence of commitment to the church's historic creeds and confessions.[3] But as Machen said, 'In the presence of a great common foe, I have little time to be attacking my brethren who stand with me in defence of the word of God.' As for labels, he affirmed: 'What I prefer to call myself is not a

[3] Machen was always remarkably free of cultural taboos, possessing a strong independence of thought that sometimes put him at odds with the prevalent attitudes of the day. For example, he opposed Prohibition when virtually all evangelicals approved it, approved of the movies (he was a Charlie Chaplin fan) when almost all evangelicals condemned it, and sympathised with Germany during the First World War when almost all Americans were anti-German.

"Fundamentalist" but a "Calvinist"—that is, an adherent of the Reformed Faith. As such I regard myself as standing in the great central current of the church's life—the current that flows down from the word of God through Augustine and Calvin.'

Machen's contributions to the Fundamentalist side of the controversy included his scholarly defence of the supernatural character of the apostle Paul's religion (*The Origin of Paul's Religion,* 1921), of the virgin birth (*The Virgin Birth of Christ,* 1930), *The Christian Faith in the Modern World,* and *The Christian View of Man* (both 1935, originally radio lectures that year), and his masterpiece *Christianity and Liberalism* (1923). His central thesis in the last-named work was to critique the liberal version of Christianity as, in reality, not being the Christian religion at all, but a different man-made religion, since it denied all Christianity's basic supernatural and historic tenets. Machen did not want to deprive liberals of their civil liberties; they were entirely free to practise their liberalism. But in the name of honesty, they must stop pretending it was Christianity. He especially detested what he looked upon as the rank insincerity of men subscribing to creeds and confessions which they manifestly did not believe, and torturing the language of those creeds to make them mean something no honest person could think they really meant.

The liberal controversy spilled over into Machen's seminary and church. As liberalism made increasing inroads into Princeton, Machen led an exodus from the seminary in 1929 to form a new theological training school, Westminster Seminary, whose tutors included famous apologist Cornelius Van Til (1895–1987), systematic theologian John Murray (1898–1975), and Old Testament scholar O. T. Allis (1880–1973). Westminster became and remains the single most influential Reformed seminary in the world.

When in Machen's perception liberalism made analogous inroads into American Presbyterianism, he found he could no longer conscientiously support his church's official missionary program—it was sending out 'missionaries' who did not have the true gospel to proclaim. His first response was to use his wealth to fund a new independent missionary program, rooted in historic credal Christianity; but his liberal-controlled denomination tried him for 'insubordination,' deposing him from its ministry in 1934. With a body of sympathisers, Machen established the Orthodox Presbyterian Church in 1936.[4] The OPC continues to this day, faithful to the vision of Christianity that had gripped Machen.

Machen died relatively young of pneumonia on New Year's Day 1937, at the age of fifty-five. He never married, and in some ways led a solitary, perhaps lonely life.[5] However,

[4] It was originally called the Presbyterian Church of America, but legal complications resulted in its changing its name to the Orthodox Presbyterian Church.

[5] The only woman to whom he was in any sense attracted was a highly cultured Unitarian. The differences in religion between them proved an impassable barrier.

his outstanding championship of historic Christianity and the Reformed faith during the Fundamentalist-Modernist controversy has left an abiding legacy, in his writings, in Westminster Seminary, and in the Orthodox Presbyterian Church. Perhaps the noblest tribute to Machen at the time of his death came from journalist H. L. Mencken (1880–1956), well-known for his acidic witticisms, and no friend of orthodox Christianity; yet Mencken was a great friend of honesty and learning, and affirmed in his obituary of Machen that both qualities had been on Machen's side in the Fundamentalist-Modernist conflict:

> He was actually a man of great learning, and, what is more, of sharp intelligence. What caused him to quit the Princeton Theological Seminary and found a seminary of his own was his complete inability, as a theologian, to square the disingenuous evasions of Modernism with the fundamentals of Christian doctrine. He saw clearly that the only effects that could follow diluting and polluting Christianity in the Modernist manner would be its complete abandonment and ruin. Either it was true or it was not true. If, as he believed, it was true, then there could be no compromise with persons who sought to whittle away its essential postulates, however respectable their motives.
>
> Thus he fell out with the reformers who have been trying, in late years, to convert the Presbyterian Church into a kind of literary and social club, devoted vaguely to good works. Most of the other Protestant churches

have gone the same way, but Dr Machen's attention, as a Presbyterian, was naturally concentrated upon his own connection. His one and only purpose was to hold it [the Church] resolutely to what he conceived to be the true faith. When that enterprise met with opposition he fought vigorously, and though he lost in the end and was forced out of Princeton it must be manifest that he marched off to Philadelphia [home of Westminster Seminary] with all the honours of war.

BANNER *of* TRUTH

The Banner of Truth Trust originated in 1957 in London. The founders believed that much of the best literature of historic Christianity had been allowed to fall into oblivion and that, under God, its recovery could well lead not only to a strengthening of the church, but to true revival.

Interdenominational in vision, this publishing work is now international, and our lists include a number of contemporary authors, together with classics from the past. The translation of these books into many languages is encouraged.

A monthly magazine, *The Banner of Truth*, is also published, and further information about this, and all our other publications, may be found on our website, banneroftruth.org, or by contacting the offices below:

Head Office:
3 Murrayfield Road
Edinburgh
EH12 6EL
United Kingdom
Email: info@banneroftruth.co.uk

North America Office:
610 Alexander Spring Road
Carlisle, PA 17015
United States of America
Email: info@banneroftruth.org